# BestCredit

# BestCredit

## HOW TO WIN THE CREDIT GAME

Learn from a collection agency insider

DANA A. NEAL

PALADIN PRESS
BOULDER, COLORADO

*BestCredit: How to Win the Credit Game*
by Dana A. Neal

Copyright © 2003 by Dana A. Neal

ISBN 1-58160-418-1
Printed in the United States of America

Published by Paladin Press, a division of
Paladin Enterprises, Inc.
Gunbarrel Tech Center
7077 Winchester Circle
Boulder, Colorado 80301 USA
+1.303.443.7250

Direct inquiries and/or orders to the above address.

Visit our Web site at www.paladin-press.com

# TABLE OF

▲

# CONTENTS

# ▲
# DISCLAIMER

This book provides information on techniques the reader can use to improve credit and/or reduce debt. Those actions are the full and total responsibility of the individual, and no guarantees or warrantees are provided. It is the responsibility of the reader to evaluate the accuracy, completeness, or usefulness of any information, opinion, or other content available in this book; check with an attorney and review your state laws. The author is not engaged in rendering any legal service. The services of a professional attorney are recommended if legal advice or assistance is needed. The author and publisher disclaim any responsibility for personal loss or liabilities caused by the use or misuse of any information presented herein.

▲

# FOREWORD

Most consumers don't even
realize the impact their everyday
behavior has on their credit standing, and thus their everyday lives. As
a loan officer at a mortgage broker-
age firm, I see people every day who
are affected in various ways by their
credit rating. There are those who
are in excellent standing and have
the best rates, programs, and services available to them, and then
there are those who pay a premium
for their loan—or don't qualify at
all—based on their credit report.

Many of you already know that
when you want to do anything in
life, the people who are in a position
to help you will likely use a critical
eye and look at three things: credit,
character, and collateral. Otherwise
known as the Three Cs, they're all

connected, but the first two are deeply connected, since prevailing perceptions are that you can't have one without the other. That's why *BestCredit* is so important, because fixing your credit will prop up the perception of character and then, over time, the collateral will follow.

The reality is that a good credit score is achievable for everyone! As you'll soon discover, *BestCredit* takes the guesswork out of the credit scoring process and provides a clear, methodical plan to making your credit the best it can be. It's the most comprehensive program that I've seen for reestablishing credit or improving your score.

The opportunity to work with the author on my own credit improvement plan and preview *BestCredit* has been a tremendous asset to me, not only personally but professionally as well. The ability to effectively advise my clients on how they can improve their scores is no small thing, and it's rewarding to see them empowered—obtaining the financing they need to accomplish their life goals.

Dana Neal's frankness and clarity are not only refreshing, but they make the information in *BestCredit* easy to understand, digest, and implement. His use of specific, real-life examples lets you know that this former bill collector really *knows* what he's talking about. Furthermore, he brings a certain class to a genre that's filled with unsavory characters and dubious advice.

If you are the type that cuts corners or skims paragraphs, don't do it. There's much to know and many nuances, but the breadth and depth of information are a positive testament to the thoroughness of this book.

Once you've applied the tools the author provides, apologies or excuses for your credit will never again be necessary.

—T.J. Mehan, Loan Officer
Consumer Financial

▲

# PREFACE

First and foremost, I wish to commend you for taking steps to improve your credit and reduce debt. It demonstrates initiative on your part and a commitment to improving your credit situation. This will ultimately enhance not only your credit but your life.

As you'll soon learn, it's this commitment—mixed with perseverance and the tools I'll provide—that is the key to attaining your goals. Within this book, you'll uncover the recipe for success, and you'll be a force to be reckoned with.

And yet it's easy to feel bad when your credit is poor; a bad report is often accompanied by guilt, shame, and even depression. And every time you get denied, it's a sobering reminder of an old mistake—a festering wound. But don't be disheartened, because you'll begin to feel better just as soon as you act to do something about it.

Doing something begins with learning and having an open mind. Many people are misinformed about their rights concerning debt collections, credit reporting, and debt reduction. As a former bill collector, I learned firsthand the cold, hard facts about debtors and creditors. Having been on both ends of the spectrum, I have gained a keen understanding of the many facets of credit reporting and the many tools that are available to get you out of trouble. My goal is to arm you with this knowledge in order to turn things around and get you going on the right track. Each method that I present is tried and true; there isn't anything in the book that I haven't tried personally.

It's my belief that credit reporting is inherently flawed. Why? Because there are extenuating, life-altering circumstances that often lead to financial changes and thus financial risk. These occurrences are often outside the control of individual persons. Yes, the credit reporting system is there for lending institutions to assess risk when extending credit, but the risk assessment and the credit extended are based on a set of circumstances that can ultimately change. Yes, an individual's "creditworthiness" may have changed, but only as a function of how much credit to extend, not whether or not he or she is actually a good credit risk.

A rational financial risk assessment process is not linear, as life-altering events can change the equation. A loan officer looking at an individual's creditworthiness after he or she has suffered a financial disaster, in effect, does not see the same person that another creditor saw when extending credit to that individual prior to the disaster. Creditors should take past credit history into account when assessing current and future risk, but they don't; they only see the current credit report. This seems patently unfair and unrealistic. The current system of credit reporting only concerns itself with whether or not a debt was paid and when. The underlying assumption is that people either pay or don't pay based on their character (and all that this entails).

This measure of creditworthiness is far too simplistic, which is one of the reasons I wrote *BestCredit*! It is intended to serve as the great equalizer, since it provides the tools necessary to balance out the inherent flaws of the credit reporting system.

It's disturbing just how brutal negative credit can be—it can leave you paralyzed! Even a small amount of negative credit can affect what interest rate you pay on you car or home loan, so it's important to make your credit perfect, or at least the best it can be. This book will show you how to 1) understand credit reporting and improve your score, 2) remove negative credit, whether factual or not, 3) remove inquiries, 4) reestablish credit, 5) establish years of good credit where none existed, 6) identify bad credit repair techniques that are purported by other sources, 7) draft concise and effective letters to creditors and credit reporting agencies (CRAs), 8) put collectors in their place, 9) understand and restore your overall privacy, 10) get 25 to 75 percent taken off of your debt, 11) remove judgments, 12) know how and when to find and use an attorney, 13) prevent and recover from identity theft, and much more. It will also address many subtle, little-known issues like tax consequences of settlements and charge-offs. *BestCredit* is about covering all of the bases—reestablishing and repairing credit simultaneously, reducing debt, and using your rights to your advantage in order to take your credit rating to a higher level very quickly. All you need to do is follow the guidelines that I lay out for you, and your credit will soon be the best it can be, and more than likely flawless.

The information contained within this book is very comprehensive, and it's important that you read each section carefully so that you can apply the various techniques in the most effective manner. Each individual's situation is unique. Those who learn the most will be the most effective at applying the methods to their particular situation. Although there are many strategies and examples given, the ideal student of credit improvement will take from this book a great deal more than just an ability to apply a solution to any particular type of credit problem. He or she will be able to devise techniques independently. Although there are many great answers found within these pages, there is no substitute for improvising, being creative, and using a new spin on an old wheel. This "alchemy" will allow you to formulate the most potent mixture for use in your own individual circumstance.

Again, the information I provide here is based on my own experience, both as a collector and a debtor. Keep in mind that my mission is not to make judgments about decisions regarding your credit—right or wrong, ethical or unethical. I'm simply the purveyor of the information that will enable you to make an informed decision. Every situation is unique, and you must decide for yourself who to pay, who not to pay, how much, and under what terms.

There are various other books available on the subject of credit repair, many of which offer flow charts or tables that illustrate your prospective chances at negative credit removal based on factors like patterns of lateness, type of debt, and so on. This may all look interesting, but the bottom line is this: *every item that is derogatory has a high probability for removal*. The major factor that will affect your success rate is how well you learn the lessons contained within this book.

It's important to me that readers not only have success in their quest for perfect credit and debt reduction, but that they also feel that *BestCredit* really helped them improve their lives. If you have any ideas on how to improve upon the information provided here, you may e-mail me at info@bestcredit.com. Of course, I get many e-mails and cannot respond to every one, but I do read all of them. You may also log on to www.bestcredit.com and see what new products and services are available.

▲

# CHAPTER 1

# THE RULES
# OF THE GAME

I've laid out a plan that is methodical and realistic. If you wish to jump to a particular section, that's entirely up to you, but you'd be remiss in doing so. Be assured, every word, every rule has a purpose. If this is going to work for you, you need to get serious and now.

You must be adequately prepared to make a good evaluation of your individual situation. This evaluation will likely look very different after you've finished this book, which is why reading carefully is so important. You should be receptive to the many possibilities.

Let's get started with the rules of the game:

1) *Start paying your bills on time, period.* Never, under any circumstances, pay your bills late.

2) *Start paying your bills on time, period.* Even if you have to "borrow from Peter to pay Paul," never, under any circumstances, pay your bills late. (Bear in mind that moving debt around between creditors can negatively affect your score, but not nearly as much as paying late. Of course this assumes that each creditor to which you are moving debt reports on the same report.)

3) *Start paying your bills on time, period.* Bad credit is brutal, isn't it? The whole idea is to put as much distance as you can between you and your bad credit. The way you do this is to pay your bills on time, starting now!

4) *If you blame anyone else for your situation, stop it now.* Forget the crappie boss, the bitter spouse who wouldn't pay the bills, the unforeseen medical problems, and so on. It doesn't matter why; it's past, and you need to take responsibility for now to move forward.

5) *Stop feeling bad.* Yes, while the feelings that often accompany bad credit— hopelessness, guilt, stress, and worse— are often painful, the first step to feeling better is to do something about it. You're doing that right now, so you'll begin to feel better as you take control.

6) *Know your rights under the Fair Credit Reporting Act (FCRA).* The FCRA is designed to help ensure that CRAs furnish correct and complete information to businesses to use when evaluating your application.

## YOUR RIGHTS UNDER THE FCRA

- You have the right to receive a copy of your credit report. The copy of your report must contain all of the information in your file at the time of your request.
- You have the right to know the name of anyone who received your credit report in the last year for most purposes or in the last two years for employment purposes.
- Any company that denies your application must supply the name and address of the CRA it contacted, provided the denial was based on information obtained from the CRA.

- You have the right to a free copy of your credit report when your credit application is denied because of information supplied by the CRA. Your request for your report must be made within 60 days of receiving your denial notice.
- If you contest the completeness or accuracy of information contained in your report, you should file a dispute with the CRA and with the company that furnished the information to the CRA. Both the CRA and the furnisher of the information are legally obligated to reinvestigate your dispute.

The complete text of the Fair Credit Reporting Act can be found in Appendix C.

7) *If you haven't already, order a copy of all three credit reports, and make sure you understand them.* You can learn more about understanding them in the next chapter. Be sure and read the documentation that comes along with them, since their formats often change. Get three file folders, a highlighter, and a small box of two-holed prong paper fasteners (from Office Depot, Office Max, or any office supply store). Label the folders Experian, Trans Union, and Equifax. Place each of the respective credit reports in these folders on the left side, and place two-holed prongs on the right for your future correspondence. (The highlighter is for marking this book with important information so you can easily reference it later.)

## HOW TO GET YOUR CREDIT REPORTS

There are three CRAs in the United States. Although you may have a local CRA, local agencies are merely affiliates that get their information from one of the three main CRAs listed here:

### Equifax
P.O. Box 740241
Atlanta, Georgia 30374-0241
www.equifax.com

**4**

**Trans Union**
P.O. Box 403
Springfield, PA 19064
www.transunion.com

**Experian** (Formerly TRW)
P.O. Box 2104
Allen, TX 75013-2104
www.experian.com

When you order a copy of your report by mail, be sure to include the following in your request:

- Full name (including Jr., Sr., II)
- Social Security number
- Current address
- Date of birth
- Signature
- Telephone number (home)
- Copy of utility bill (to the address where you are requesting that the report be sent)
- A check or money order for the amount charged for the report, if applicable

> *Caution:* If you're currently having problems with bill collectors or expect to, you'll want to read the section on "getting lost" before you do this. Giving your private information to the CRA is equivalent to handing it to the entire world—including collectors.

As of 2001, you can use a major credit card to order and view your reports online with the CRAs' respective Web sites.

> *Tip:* Be careful with online reports. Some of these CRA Web sites only permit you to view your report once, so be sure to print it out. You can also hit FILE/SAVE in your Web, saving the Web page to your hard drive for later viewing.

Credit reporting agencies charge you approximately $9.50 for a copy of your report. (Or $12 if you want your report and your score. This is unjust and a loophole in the law . . . they're just squeezing consumers for more money until Congress does something about it; but you'll want your score so you can track your progress.) It's important that you also include a copy of a utility bill that has your current address on it. That way they can verify who you are the first time around and you won't get any letters asking you to prove who you are before your report can be provided.

> **Note:** Some states have special laws that permit consumers to have rights and recourses not available to those in other states. For example, under Connecticut law your report may not exceed $5 for the first disclosure and $7.50 thereafter. If you've disputed an item with a CRA, Connecticut also allows for you to request the company name, address, and telephone number of anyone contacted during the investigation. Colorado has some interesting laws: get one free copy of your report per year, and get a free copy if you've had 8 or more inquiries in the past 12 months or if you've had any negative information added to your report. In addition, some states have higher penalties for civil action brought against those who unlawfully obtain a copy of their report. The states with additional laws are Connecticut, California, Colorado, Maryland, Massachusetts, Vermont, and Washington. Log onto http://www.experian.com/yourcredit/index.html and click "All About Credit" and then "FCRA Rights" for more information, or check with your state's attorney general.

If you've been denied credit within the last 60 days, a copy of your report is free. Simply send a copy of your denial letter to the respective address shown. Another way to get a "free" copy is to go online to one of the many companies that offer free credit reports. Be advised, however, you will pay a price in privacy, since your information will be sold to hundreds of scummy marketers; not worth it if you ask me.

> **Note:** CRAs are notorious for stalling and will use whatever means necessary to prevent their having to do something. The most common delay tactic is to respond to your letter asking you to verify that "you are who you say you are" by sending them another request and including a copy of a utility bill in order to verify your address. They shouldn't require this (and would probably get spanked if it was challenged in court), but this is not the battle to fight. In your first correspondence, always include a copy of a bill (one with the address of the location to which you want the file sent). For those wishing to be "lost," use a bill that has been sent to your P.O. Box, not to your home address. If you use your home address, it will end up on your report, and the creditor will have found you. Again, for more about being lost (but not running), refer to the section on "getting lost" in Chapter 4: Dealing with Collectors.

### Other Types of Credit Reports

In addition to consumer credit reports, there are two other types of credit reports: infiles and full factual.

### Infiles

An infile is far more complete (and sometimes more useful for credit repair) than a consumer credit report, and it's what professional lenders will see. Lenders are not permitted to show you this file, and the only way you can get it is to register yourself as a landlord or employer with the CRA. It's easy, requiring a simple application that you can fax to the CRA once you've filled it out. I recommend that you use a company name to get registered, and an LLC or corporation is even better.

Once you've registered your company, have someone who works for your company pull an infile on you. The cost for this is often actually less than that of a consumer credit report!

There may be an advantage to having these in hand, since there may be something on there that your consumer credit report doesn't display.

### Full Factual Credit Reports

Also known as a residential mortgage report, they're used when applying for a home loan. It's nothing more than two infiles from two separate CRAs, and they can be from any combination of CRAs. If you want to see this, your best course is to get the infiles from all three CRAs, and then you'll be sure to have everything you need.

These reports are prepared by subcontractors to the CRAs. As service bureaus, they do the legwork of verifying information about you (e.g., salary, address, etc.)

Some credit repair "professionals" claim that going through the service bureaus is useful, since they are much faster at correcting information. As I see it, this is a waste of time, since correcting service bureau reports will not correct those on file with the three CRAs. (The CRAs refuse to use service bureau reports as a basis for correction, and good luck trying to make them do so.) And these days, mortgage brokers and the like will often pull a quick preliminary credit report from one of the main CRAs before they do anything else.

Let's continue now with the rules of the game:

8) *Get some blank sheets of paper and begin writing down the following notes for each individual report*:

  a. Negative information that is inaccurate.
     (This is usually the easiest to repair.)
  b. Positive information that should be included
     but isn't.
  c. Negative information that is accurate.

(For further explanation of negative and positive information, refer to Chapter 2: Understanding Your Report, under the section on deciphering your report.) Each credit report will often contain different items. In some cases, a negative item may be found on one report but not on the others. This also holds true with positive information. Don't worry about this, as you will treat each report as separate in many respects. By disregarding all of the confusing ancillary data that accompanies the reports, this exercise gives you a sense of what it is you're dealing with by helping to clarify exactly what needs to be addressed. Thus it's easier to analyze, prioritize, and *grasp*.

9) *Prioritize.* This is where you "make your money," so to speak. Both time and energy are required to improve things, so you must focus your efforts where you can make the most headway in the shortest amount of time. Begin by attacking those things that will have the highest degree of success and can be accomplished the fastest. Usually, the order in which credit issues should be approached is as follows:

   a. Reestablish your credit. This can be done two ways. The first is by always paying your current open accounts on time. The second is by opening up one or two new accounts in order to create accounts with a perfect history. (More on this in Chapter 5: Things You Can Do Right Now to Improve Your Score.)
   b. Add positive information that should be reported, but isn't, to your report.
   c. Establish years of good credit where none existed. This technique will enable you to create an account on your credit file that wasn't there before. It's useful for people with little or no credit, or for those with very few good account entries on their credit report. (See Chapter 5 for a detailed explanation.)
   d. Remove information that is negative, but false, from your report.

e. Remove information that is negative, but true, from
your report.
f. Remove judgments.
g. Remove inquiries.

**Note:** This order may seem strange at first, but
there are two primary factors to consider when determining what your priorities are. The first is what is eas-
iest to get changed or added, and the second is what
will have the greatest impact on your score. For example, it's really easy to open another account, and it's
hardest to get judgments removed. Yet inquiries don't
affect your score as much, so they are listed after
judgments.

Keep in mind that this is a guide, not a set of hard-and-
fast rules. Only you can determine your priorities because
only you know your circumstance. Which problems are the
most pressing? Are you about to lose a house or car? Are you
about to get sued for failed credit card payments? All of us are
busy, and surely you won't spend time opening new accounts
when you're about to lose your car. Think about it very carefully, and while weighing the impact of each individual mark
on your overall score, take action relevant to your situation
that will produce the largest improvement to your report in
the shortest possible time. Go for the worst first. For example,
if your report shows a "Paid Was 60 x 2" (where 60 is the
number of days late and x 2 is the number of times past 60),
this is more harmful than a "Paid Was 30 x 2." So go after the
former first. Another example: If you have two different
accounts that are equally negative, and one is reported with
only one CRA whereas the other the other is reported with
two or three, go after the latter. If you have negative items that
vary widely in dollar amounts, you may want to go after the
ones that are the smallest if you're short of capital. A more
recent lateness is more harmful than an older one, so go for
improving the reporting on the newer account.

Consider ahead of time that it may take some cash to get you out of one or more of your circumstances. But fortunately, with unsecured debt (that which is not secured by collateral), you can usually get the amount that you owe reduced by as much as 75 percent. Perhaps debt reduction is your main goal. Only you can decide, but you'll have a better idea once you fully understand your report and have absorbed this book.

10) *Attack anything on your credit that is negative, period. No matter how small it appears!* Keep in mind that even a little thing can affect what interest rate you pay on all types of loans.
11) *Learn the art of negotiation.* This is covered in detail in Chapter 3.
12) *In all of your contacts with creditors, collectors, and CRAs, be nice!* It will go a long, long way. Even if you get the wrong answer, be nice. Trust me. I know what I'm talking about. I recommend a fabulous book, which has sold millions of copies, called *How to Win Friends and Influence People*, by Dale Carnegie. It will serve you well for this project and for all future endeavors.
13) *Always use the insurance method in your dealings with creditors, collectors, and CRAs.* This means that you get things in writing, and when you send something to them, send it by certified mail, return receipt requested. This prevents their backpedaling, or ignoring you entirely, when it's time for them to do something that they promised or are required by law to do. It's also useful when filing suit. Make sure that in all of your contacts, you keep a log of whom you spoke with (full name, phone number, and extension), the time, and the date. Begin every conversation by politely asking for a name (first and last). If you can't get a last name, get the last initial or operator number and geographical location. It can also be useful to get an e-mail address, since people are apt to say things via e-mail they wouldn't normally say, and e-mail provides you with a record of the correspondence. (Yes, e-mails have been shown to be admissible in court!)

14) *Know ahead of time what you're going to do if a creditor goes back on a deal.* What do you do if a creditor goes back on a deal you have in writing? Well, that's your business, but personally I'd get a good lawyer and sue. When creditors make deals in writing and then break them, taking legal action can force them to own up to their agreements. If you can, stipulate a venue in the written agreements with creditors, namely your state. This will make it easier for you to litigate should it be required. (You may want to sue as a plaintiff in *pro se*, representing yourself; more on that in the "dealing with creditors" section later.)

15) *Make sure that you get corrected copies of your credit report each time something is improved* (corrected copies are free). As you go along, you'll find that the CRAs will make changes to your report. Put the old files in another folder and label it "credit archives" in order to avoid confusion. (If you ever need to file suit, they'll also come in handy.) Put copies of correspondence with creditors on the right side of the folders, keeping all of them.

▲

# CHAPTER 2

# UNDERSTANDING YOUR REPORT

It's important to note that each CRA uses different formats for its reports, and they change their formats every few years. As a result, it doesn't make sense for me to explain a format, only to have it change next week! When you order a copy of your reports, they will be sent to you along with an explanation sheet. However, they are similar in many ways, and the terminology is generally universal.

## DECIPHERING YOUR REPORT

In a nutshell, there are items on your report that a lender will view as neutral, positive, or negative:

### Neutral
- Paid
- Refinanced

**13**

- Credit Card Lost
- Unrated (won't affect score, but human eyes may not like it)
- Current Was 30 (x 1 in the last 12 months)
- Paid Was 30
- Inquiry (a reasonable number is okay, but the fewer the better)

### Positive

- Paid Never Late
- Paid as Agreed
- Account Current
- Account Closed by Consumer (you)

### Negative

- Current Was 30 [Days Late]
- Current Was 60/90/120 [Days Late]
- Paid Was 60/90/120 [Days Late]
- Repossession (the item was taken back by the creditor)
- Charge-Off (creditor doesn't expect to collect and has probably filed for a tax deduction)
- Paid Charge-Off (same as charge-off, but balance paid)
- Delinquent
- BK (bankruptcy)
- Inc in BK (written off in a bankruptcy)
- Collection Account (creditor has turned over or sold debt at a discount to a collection agency)
- Paid Collection (paid collection account)
- SCNL (subscriber cannot locate, meaning you skipped)
- Acct Closed at Granter's Request (creditor closed the account)
- Judgment (you were sued by the creditor and lost)
- Tax Lien (unpaid back taxes)
- Settled (you were late and paid a portion; weighted less if it wasn't recent)
- Inquiry (3 or more in the preceding 12 months)

There is no need to be intimidated by all of the information on a report. Just focus in on the status, and look in the area below the status to see if the account was ever reported late, e.g., "3 times 90 days." You will see a key indicator on some mailed reports, a two- to three-character (letter-number or letter-number-number) identifier for every account. The letter is for the type of account (e.g., revolving, installment), while the ending number is for the status. Each CRA has a status for the account (it is here that you can find the rating). The status can be a simple phrase, like "Paid Never Late" and/or it can be a number from 0 to 9. "0" is unrated, "1" is current, and "9" is a charge-off or bad debt.

These numbers will be preceded by the type of credit in the form of a letter:

- R = Revolving (payment amount variable)
- C = Checking line of credit
- O = Open account (entire balance due each month)
- I = Installment (fixed number of payments)

The numbers that come after the letters are one of the most important aspects of your accounts, and they mean the following:

- R00 or UR = Revolving, unrated (approved but unused or too new to rate)
- I01 = Installment, paid as agreed
- I02 = Installment, 30+ days late
- I03 = Installment, 60+ days late
- O04 = Open, 90+ days late
- I05 = Installment 120+ days late; or collection account
- R06 = Revolving, 150 days late
- R07 = Making regular payments under wage earner plan or similar arrangement
- I08 = Repossession
- R09 = Revolving, seriously delinquent/charge-off to bad debt (can be paid or unpaid)

The online reports often differ from the printed ones that you get in the mail, which is why it pays to simply get the CRA's current explanation sheet and familiarize yourself with it.

> **Note:** How does your report get pulled? Those whom you are doing business with have the right to pull your credit file, period. Providing them with a Social Security number equals your implicit approval of the inquiry. It's just that simple. Many creditors will have direct accounts with CRAs, so they may get it that way. Others will use third parties, such as associations, to get it for them, and in many cases they don't even have to be member in order to pull it; simply pay a fee per file. In all cases, they can pull one or more CRA files in order to assess your creditworthiness.

You should make an attempt to remove from your report any account that is not positive or neutral, no matter how seemingly small the amount or infraction.

## THINGS THAT WILL OFTEN GET YOU DENIED

When you are applying for credit, the following items will often cause your application to be denied when they appear on your report:

- Past 30 days two or more times or past 60 in the last 12 months or worse
- A bankruptcy in the last 10 years (Chapter 7 or 13)
- Judgment against you in the last 7 years (any length of time is bad if it's unpaid)
- Excessive number of inquiries (more than three in one year)
- No hard address (P.O. Box only)
- No telephone
- No credit references
- Less than 12 months at your current job
- Large debt-to-income ratio

- Large number of revolving accounts (i.e., credit cards, over-draft protection, and home equity line of credit; each has a minimum payment and the credit can be accessed repeatedly)
- Large number of revolving credit cards
- No bank accounts (checking or savings)
- Self-employed with unsubstantiated income (usually they want to see tax returns for the last two years)

A review of credit scoring (below) will reveal what other factors can influence a potential lender in determining whether to extend credit or not. Often your credit can be perfect, but you will still be denied if you have excessive inquires or have been extended a large amount of credit relative to your income.

*Tip:* Think very hard before you respond to that "6 months same as cash!" offer. Every such response will result in an inquiry appearing on your credit report and could sabotage your chance at getting that new car or home loan!

*Caution:* When you give someone your Social Security number, you are by default authorizing that person to pull your credit file, and the inquiry may hurt your score.

Lenders weigh negative credit based on when it occurred. For example, if you had a judgment a few years ago that is now paid, you'll be better off than if it was within the last year. It's important for you to always pay your bills on time so you can get approved nearly every time you apply for credit.

### How Long Does Negative Information Stay on Your Report?

Knowing when the clock begins and ends for bad credit is very useful when trying to decide whom to pay, how much, and when. Consider the following carefully:

- Bankruptcies stay on the report for 10 years.
- All other negative items, even charge-offs, stay on the report for 7 years from the time the account went delinquent. If it was a charge-off, then it is reported 7 years from the date the charge-off occurred. (It could be 7 years from the last transaction . . . more on that in a later chapter.) There are some exceptions to the 7-year rule, however. (Lenders will notify the CRA if the consumer's credit request meets these criteria, and in such cases the CRA *will* report negative items that are more than 7 years old.):
- When a consumer attempts to get a loan for $150,000 or greater, there's no time limit. For those wanting to own a home in the future, this is yet another reason to get those bad items removed.
- Information reported because of an application for a job with a salary of more than $75,000 has no time limit.
- Information reported because of an application for more than $150,000 worth of life insurance has no time limit.
- Federal law says judgments can remain for 7 years or the length of the state statute. Judgments stay for 5 years in Ohio, renewable indefinitely; 10 years in Oregon, renewable once for 10 more years; other states are just as bad.
- (Can anything be worse than indefinite?) Always be cognizant of this and avoid judgments when practical. Even a Chapter 7 bankruptcy can be preferable, since it drops off in 10 years, and you can obtain new, desirable credit in after just two!
- Student Loans. The Higher Education Act of 1965, section 430(a)(f), reads as follows:

(f) DURATION OF AUTHORITY.—Notwithstanding paragraphs (4) and (6) of subsection (a) of section 605 of the Fair Credit Reporting Act (15 U.S.C. 1681c (a)(4), (a)(6)), a consumer reporting agency may make a report containing information received from the Secretary or a guaranty agency, eligible lender, or subsequent holder regarding the status of a borrower's defaulted account on a loan guaranteed under this part

until—
 (1) 7 years from the date on which the Secretary or the agency paid a claim to the holder on the guaranty;
 (2) 7 years from the date the Secretary, guaranty agency, eligible lender, or subsequent holder first reported the account to the consumer reporting agency; or
 (3) in the case of a borrower who reenters repayment after defaulting on a loan and subsequently goes into default on such loan, 7 years from the date the loan entered default such subsequent time.

Just bear in mind that the 7-year clock begins when one of these things occurs, not when you first default on the student loan.

*It is important to understand how these reporting rules affect your individual report.* This is further expounded upon in Chaper 6: Removing Information that Is Negative, but True, in the section on analyzing your situation before you act.

 ***Tip:*** *Joint accounts (i.e., credit extended in the name of two or more parties) create the potential for all sorts of problems. Where people and relationships are involved, unforeseen complications often arise. Therefore, it's best to keep all of your credit cards separate—even from your mate. Ever heard a divorcee say, "My ex ruined my credit . . . damn it." Of course you have, and having joint accounts is the number-one reason this happens. More importantly, in some states, once you use someone else's credit card, you're liable for the entire balance—no matter how much you charged and what the balance was at the time you used it. (This is at least true in the state of Ohio and may be in your state as well.) For this and other reasons that go beyond the scope of this book, you should never use another person's credit card, no matter what the circumstance.*

## CREDIT SCORING

There are several things that are looked at in credit scoring models, and not all lenders use the same models. Credit bureau scores are often called "FICO scores" because most credit bureau scores used in the United States are produced from software developed by Fair Isaac and Company. The FICO score is the most widely used, but all scoring models are important (though payment history is the most important). Lenders often use their own scoring models, known as custom models.

> **Note:** All CRAs use the FICO scoring model, but they call it something different. Equifax's is "BEACON," Experian's is "Experian/Fair Isaac Risk Model," and Trans Union's is EMPIRICA. Don't be alarmed when the scores from each CRA are different. It just means that accounts either didn't show up on each report or were reported differently. (This can be a good thing, since a negative account may only show up on one report.)

A FICO score ranges from 300 to 850, and assuming that your debt-to-income ratio is within a lender's limits, a 620+ meets the secondary market guidelines and will get you approved with mainstream lenders. A 720+ will get you the best interest rates, and 500–619 will get you a B and C loan (alternative loan that doesn't meet secondary market guidelines—the interest rate will be higher). The exception is if you had a bankruptcy within the last year. Even if your score is within an acceptable range, you'll usually be declined by B and C lenders , and for 24 months by mainstream lenders, for 12 months following a bankruptcy.

For a FICO score to be calculated, your credit report must contain at least one account that has been open for six months or more and at least one account that has been updated in the past six months. Here are the primary factors used for scoring:

- Previous payment history
- Your age
- Monthly obligations relative to income
- Account balances relative to income
- Years at current address
- Age of credit file
- Types of credit previously issued (many types are better than only one, particularly if all are secured. A combination of unsecured credit cards and installment loans are best; and a mortgage if you already own a home).

**Note:** As stated previously, moving around debt between creditors (who are reporting) can reduce your score, so you'll want to be careful about this.

Pending legislation H.R. 1176 Fair Credit Reporting Act Amendments of 2001 will require CRAs to provide detailed information about credit scoring models to consumers. But until then, the important thing to remember is that if an item is not positive or neutral, it negatively affects your score.

Lenders will use different criteria for different situations. Unsecured debt is riskier than secured debt in general since there's no collateral involved in unsecured debt. You see, it's all about "what happens if you default?" A house or auto is collateral, and if you default, then the lender can always come and take it—mitigating its loss. If you're getting a good deal on a car and putting money down, you have a better chance than if you're paying above book value and putting no money down. Once again, if they repossess the car due to nonpayment, then they can mitigate their loss if there's equity in the car. Further, a college student with no prior credit history may be given more of a chance than someone who is 30-something and has no history.

If you've done business with the lender's bank (i.e., they have extended credit to you previously or you have a checking/savings account with them), it helps. It also helps if you deal face-to-face with a loan officer at your bank, because you become more than just a name. In the last few years, however, most underwriting is not preformed by a branch, but at a corporate office—where you're just another name on a piece of paper. Some banks still can approve loans at branch level; ask the branch manager about this before you fill out an application.

> **Tip:** Let's say the consumer mortgage division of a bank has $100 million to loan. If they loan it all out, how can they continue to make loans? This is where the secondary market comes in. Once a bank makes a loan to you, they'll likely want to sell that note to the secondary market, so that they can get additional capital to loan again. The largest purchasers of these notes are the Federal Home Loan Mortgage Corporation (Freddie Mac) and the Federal National Mortgage Association (Fannie Mae). The federal government has guidelines as to what loans can qualify to be sold on the secondary market, which is why banks' hands are often tied when it comes to loan approval. It's a circle, put in place so that the lending system continues to work. There's another type of mortgage that some banks offer, called the portfolio loan. If you have bad credit but have 20 to 25 percent to put down, you can buy property under this method. There are, of course, alternative sources of home mortgage loans available to those with poor credit, but the rates are often several points higher and the terms undesirable (e.g., prepayment penalties). I don't recommend these types of loans, especially considering that if you wait and repair your credit, you can obtain conventional funding anyway.

### What FICO Says about Scoring

The following is an example of a real FICO Score Analysis. Review it carefully.

*April 17, 2001*

**Credit score:** 704
**Source of score:** Equifax (BEACON®)
**Reason codes:** 10 1 28 8

## Your BEACON score: 704

The information in your Equifax credit report has been summarized in a BEACON® score of 704. Most U.S. consumers score between 300 and 850. Generally, the higher your score, the more favorably a lender will view your application for credit. Compared to the national population, you are in the 41st percentile of consumers by credit risk. A score of 704 is somewhat below average. Studies show that for consumers with scores similar to yours, the odds of becoming seriously delinquent (90+ days past due) on one or more credit accounts are 1.72 times higher than for people with an average score.

## Understanding your percentile

Compared to the national population, your FICO® score is in the 41st percentile. This means that roughly 41% of consumers have scores lower than or equal to your own score, and 59% have scores which are higher.

## How lenders view your FICO score

Many lenders use FICO scores as one method to estimate the risk associated with an individual's application for credit. Simply put, the higher the score, the lower the risk. People with high FICO scores are proven to repay loans and credit cards more consistently than people with low FICO scores. And although the scores are remarkably accurate, no one can predict with certainty whether or not you will repay a credit account.

Frequently, there is more to consider in a credit decision than just a person's credit history. Because the FICO score is based solely on the information in your credit report, many lenders bring other factors into their decisions as well, such as your income or employment history. So the FICO score itself, while important, is by no means the only factor on which your credit application is evaluated. It is also important to understand that every lender sets their own policies and tolerance for risk when making decisions. Though many lenders incorporate FICO scores into their decisions, there is certainly no single "cutoff score" used by all lenders.

In fact, since they often consider additional information or special circumstances, some lenders may extend you credit even if your score is low, or decline your request although your score is high. Nonetheless, the FICO score is the most widely used and recognized credit rating, so it's important that you know and understand your own score.

Most lenders will view consumers with a score of 704 as an acceptable risk. This is generally recognized as a good score, and a wide array of loans and credit products will likely be available to you, often at attractive rates. Even so, remember that lenders often incorporate other information into their decision process, in addition to the FICO score, so you might be offered different rates or terms by different lenders. Nonetheless, most lenders agree that scores around 704 indicate an acceptable level of risk.

## National Distribution of FICO Scores

**Distribution.** This chart shows the percentage of people who score in specific FICO score ranges. For example, about 5% of U.S. consumers have a FICO score between 500 and 549. Your score of 704 places you in the 700–749 range, along with 20% of the total population. (Note that the score ranges shown above are provided for your information, but they do not necessarily correspond to any particular lender's policies for extending credit.)

**Credit repayment.** The second chart demonstrates the delinquency rate (or credit risk) associated with selected ranges of the FICO score. In this illustration, the delinquency rate is the percentage of borrowers who reach 90 days past due or worse on any credit account over a two-year period. For example, the delinquency rate of consumers in the 500–549 range is 71%. This means that for every 100 borrowers in this range, approximately 71 will default on a loan, file for bankruptcy, or fall 90 days past due on at least one credit account in the next two years. As a group, the consumers in your score range, 700–749, have a delinquency rate of 5%.

**Factors affecting your score.** In addition to the score, you received four reason codes. These represent the top four reasons your score was not higher. The order in which these codes were returned to you is significant: the first code represents the factor with the strongest negative impact on your score, the second code had the next strongest impact, and so on. The best way to understand how you scored and what you can do to improve your score over time is to consider these top reasons.

- *First Reason Code: 10* Your first reason code is 10, "Proportion of balances to credit limits on bank/national revolving or other revolving accounts is too high." This is the single most important factor affecting your score. Analysis of consumer credit behavior repeatedly finds that owing a substantial balance on revolving accounts relative to the amount of revolving credit available to you represents increased risk. In fact, the level of revolving debt is one of the most important factors in the FICO score. The score evaluates your total balances in relation to your total available credit on revolving accounts, as well as on individual revolving accounts. For a given amount of revolving credit available, a greater amount owed indicates a greater risk and lowers the score. (For credit cards, the total outstanding balance on your last statement is generally the amount that will show in your credit report. Note that even if you pay off your credit cards in full each and every month, your credit report may show the last billing statement balance on those accounts.)

  Paying down your revolving account balances is a good sign that you are able and willing to manage and repay your debt, and this will increase your score. On the other hand, shifting balances among revolving accounts, opening up new revolving accounts, and closing down other revolving accounts will not necessarily improve your score and could possibly decrease it.

- *Second Reason Code: 1* Your second reason code is 1, "Amount owed on accounts is too high." This is the second most important factor affecting your score. The score measures how much you owe on the accounts (revolving and installment) that are listed on your credit report. (For credit cards, the total outstanding balance on your last statement is generally the amount that will show in your credit report. Note that even if you pay off your credit cards in full each and every month, your credit report may show the last billing statement balance on those accounts.) Research reveals that consumers owing larger amounts on their credit accounts have greater future repayment risk than those who owe less. You can improve your credit score by paying off your debts. Consolidating or moving your debt around from one account to another will not, however, raise your score, since the same amount is still owed. The best advice is to pay off your debts as quickly as you can.

- *Third Reason Code: 28* Your third reason code is 28, "Number of established accounts." This reason may appear with credit reports with relatively short credit histories, but which have an unusually high number of credit accounts for such a young file. This reason may also appear with older credit files that have an unusually high number of credit accounts on file. Studies demonstrate that consumers with a relatively large number of credit accounts appearing on their credit report represent higher risk than consumers with fewer credit accounts. Therefore, avoid applying for credit you don't need or don't intend to use. (Note that closing your existing accounts will not make them disappear from your credit report immediately.) The best way to improve your credit rating is by managing *all* of your accounts responsibly and not missing any payments.

- *Fourth Reason Code: 8* Your fourth reason code is 8, "Too many inquiries last 12 months." This reason appears when your credit report contains a large number of inquiries posted as a result of your applying for credit. Research shows that consumers who are seeking several new credit accounts are riskier than consumers who are not seeking credit. Inquiries are the only information lenders have that indicates a consumer is actively seeking credit. There are different types of inquiries that reside on your credit report. The score only considers those inquiries that were posted as a result of your applying for credit. Other types of inquiries, such as promotional inquiries (where a lender has preapproved you for a credit offer) or consumer disclosure inquiries (where you have requested a copy of your own report) are not considered by the score.

  The scores can identify "rate shopping" in the mortgage- and auto-lending environment, so that one credit search involving multiple inquiries is usually only counted as a single inquiry.

Typically, the presence of inquiries on your credit file has only a small impact on FICO scores, carrying much less importance than late payments, the amount you owe, and the length of time you have used credit. This reason rarely appears as a primary or secondary reason except in high-scoring files. As time passes the age of your most recent inquiry will increase, and your score will rise as a result, provided you do not apply for additional credit in the meantime. Typically inquiries are purged from the credit bureau files after two years.

A common misperception is that every single inquiry will drop your score a certain number of points. This is not true. The impact of inquiries on your score will vary—depending on your overall credit profile. Inquiries will usually have a larger impact on the score for consumers with limited credit history and on consumers with previous late payments. The most prudent action to raise your score over time is to apply for credit *only* when you need it.

---

This example is very useful in many respects, but primarily because there aren't any derogatory items in the credit report. It's from my report, and at the time I had $250,000 in unsecured credit cards available to me! (I was receiving preapproved platinum credit card offers just about every week in the mail.) Yet FICO lists the most detrimental item as: Reason Code 10: "Proportion of balances to credit limits on bank/national revolving or other revolving accounts is too high." This is the single most important factor affecting your score. Notice that the next item listed is Reason Code 1: "Amount owed on accounts is too high." This is the second most important factor affecting your score. Next is Reason Code 28: "Number of established accounts."

Looking at this, you can see that it's absolutely critical that you do more than just remove negative items from your profile. You have to look carefully at your debt/income/balances/open accounts ratio as a whole and reorganize your finances in order to make them as streamlined as possible.

> **Tip:** *Many people take out second mortgages, or home equity loans, as a way to consolidate their debt and assist them in the streamlining process. Should you consider this route? Perhaps; it can be helpful in many respects, but it's a tool like any other—one that can be a positive or a detriment, depending on your situation. Certainly the interest rate will likely be lower than your existing debt, and the interest is tax-deductible. In this respect, debt consolidation can be beneficial, but only if you close the accounts that were consolidated so that you a) boost your score, and b) reduce your debt/payments. If you don't close your*

*other accounts, then your score may suffer even more while your overall debt goes up; many people lack the discipline to stop spending. Close the accounts and you won't have the temptation. Also, look carefully at the closing costs. If they're zero to nominal, debt consolidation will be more attractive. But don't race out and get a home equity loan until after you've read this entire book and you've found a way to maximize its benefits within your credit repair/debt reduction framework. Then do the math and determine your best course. Always remember, the credit game is a puzzle, and you, with your cunning, have to piece it together to build your masterpiece.*

***Caution:** If you opt for debt consolidation, always use a reputable lender like a bank or credit union. Again, never use alternative sources unless all other avenues have failed and you have no other choice. Most of the reasons were mentioned previously, but I'll add another: bad financial decisions look bad to reputable lenders, making them question your judgment. Also, never use a third party to perform debt consolidation. It's expensive, so why pay someone else to do what you can do yourself?*

## IN SUMMARY

- Obtain your reports from each individual CRA; get them online if you can. (Get Infiles if practicable.)
- Study your report and accompanying reference sheet. Understand what your report is telling you and prioritize. Don't bother with items that will come off of your report soon. Know your score and where you want to take it.
- Understand that a score can be impacted by more than just derogatory items.
- Don't go for B and C lending, but instead take your score to a level where you can get mainstream approval.

- All CRAs use the same FICO scoring model, but CRAs' scores may differ.
- Debt consolidation is a tool, one that can be good or bad. Very rarely does it fit, but in the unlikely event that it does fit into your scenario, remember that it takes a lot of discipline to make it work.

▲

# CHAPTER 3

# THINGS YOU MUST KNOW BEFORE YOU BEGIN PLAYING

All of the information in this book applies to anything you are trying to do, since it explains the system you are dealing with. We live in a very complex bureaucracy, and knowing the system and the human nature that accompanies it will assist you greatly.

Yet every time you have an encounter with a creditor, you will learn from the experience. In each successive encounter you will gain confidence and be better able to negotiate and cope with the "wrong" answers or the unexpected. Whatever happens, keep your cool and use reason with the person. Always remember that you are appealing to their emotions in most cases and logic to a smaller degree.

Do you have poor social skills?

If so, you will have a much harder time of it. These skills are paramount in all of your life endeavors. They require a lot of work and thought, and I believe that people aren't born with them but rather learn them. The more you work on them, the better they become, and I recommend that you constantly work to improve them. Many of us had less than stellar parents; they didn't do much to help us in the social skills department. But you can work on developing social skills everywhere you go—at the post office when dealing with clerks, in restaurants when dealing with the wait staff, at home when dealing with your kids and spouse, at work when dealing with the UPS delivery person, and so on.

## HOW TO DEAL WITH CREDITORS AND CRAS

How you talk with people is important. You must think carefully before you speak to anyone about fixing your credit. Don't ever let on that you are using a credit repair course or technique! You are just an ordinary person with a need to get that car or home loan, or whatever. If creditors or CRAs find out or suspect you are using a credit repair technique, you are likely finished because they are not going to empathize with you at that point. Remember, when dealing with creditors, appeal to their emotions.

What you owe and to whom will often dictate what approach you take with creditors. Yes, appealing to emotions is best, but if you owe money and are willing to pay the entire amount off in full in exchange for the removal of bad credit, then this gives you a strong stance from which to negotiate. On the other hand, if you don't owe any money and thus have no leverage from which to bargain, or if you are unable (or unwilling) to pay the balance, then you want to appeal to the emotions.

> *Caution:* You see it all the time—ads to "reduce your monthly payment" and "get free of debt." Companies in the credit repair and consolidation business are making money, lots of money—**your** money.

*Why would you pay someone to negotiate a lower monthly payment, only to pay him or her a fee for doing so? It makes no sense at all, particularly when you can negotiate yourself and save all of those fees. With regard to counseling, if you have trouble controlling spending and can get help from a free service in your community, by all means do it. Churches offer such services, as do government agencies and schools. Never pay for debt consolidation or credit counseling services.*

## The Art of Negotiation

The most important and fundamental element of the credit repair process is the art of negotiation. If you can learn this reasonably well, it will serve you in all things in life. An entire book can easily be devoted to the subject (and many have been). Negotiating is truly an art, and it involves understanding the following key points:

1) *Everyone wants something.*
2) *Everyone is willing to do something for that something.*
3) *You need to be able to, with reasonable accuracy, predict what that something is.*
4) *Sometimes you should just listen.* Often people will just come out and say what they will do, or they will tell you in certain nonverbal ways (excitement level, tone, etc.). Besides, listening goes a long way to building rapport.
5) *You must be good at hiding certain cards.* That is, the something you want and what you're willing to do for it must sometimes be hidden, or at least revealed in stages.
6) *Never reveal all of your cards up front.* Only reveal that which is necessary. A prospective buyer of your car doesn't need to know that you'll sell it for $8,000. It's fine if they think you'll only take $9,000 if you think they'll pay it. (This is where predicting comes in—perceiving the signs like excitement or a hurried disposition.)
7) *Engage in negotiations from a perspective of knowing what you*

*want but giving up something only in little bits and stages.* Never be in a hurry. If you want something for something, don't offer it. Offer far less. If far less doesn't work, offer a little more than far less. And if that doesn't work, tell the person you want to think about it for a few days. Try a little bit more. Go slowly.

8) *Ensure that the person with whom you are negotiating has the power to give you what you want.* You can spend months negotiating a deal, only to find that the person has no power to help you. (Yes, it happens!) The person you need to speak with doesn't answer phones for the company. In fact, he or she probably doesn't even manage the people that answer phones! The people that can help you are too important for that and are usually found in the corporate offices of the creditor. As you make your way past the many people you'll talk with in trying to find the right person, remember to be nice. You will want to pull your hair out at times, but stay calm and be persistent.

9) *Don't tell anyone who isn't in a position to help you what you are trying to do.* These people will hamper you and waste your time if you engage in specifics, and you'll usually be met with negativity. Simply explain that you wish to contact someone to discuss a problem with your report—someone with power to make changes. Indicate (nicely) that you don't wish to tell the whole story over and over again, that you wish to speak with the person who is in a position to make urgent changes. Stick to your guns, but *be nice!* (Most people you talk with won't even know who to send you to! Be prepared to go in circles, but start at corporate headquarters, the head of the collection department, or credit control. The right person is there; you just have to find him or her.) Remember, small minds and tender egos will do nothing but try to derail your efforts, since that's what small minds and tender egos do.

10) *In the case of credit repair, negotiate from the position of victim.* In most cases, you negotiate from a position of power and use logic; that is, you let the person you're negotiating with

know that you have something he or she wants. But with credit repair, I recommend this only as a last resort. Negotiating from the position of victim I find works much better. Sure, you have their money (in many cases), but they have what may amount to your new car or home loan! You will be playing or appealing to a person's compassion. It's there; you just need to find the wedge to bring it out. Don't whine, just explain to the person what happened to cause the mistake (e.g., you lost your job, you had a flood, your spouse put the screws to you) and then take responsibility by letting them know that you want to make it right! Use what I call tempered emotion, where you display a heartfelt concern but you're in control at all times.

> **Tip:** There are no hard-and-fast rules on whether to use logic or appeal to emotions when negotiating. Usually you'll use a mix of both, but the situational approach is best—that is, using a tactic that's in direct relation to the personality and demeanor of the other party. This is another area where listening can be very helpful.

11) *Make it clear that you are at fault and that you are willing to take responsibility for what happened.* Never forget this, and make this clear in your negotiations. Explain this repeatedly, and mean it! Even if your spouse ruined your credit, you married him or her, right? Sorry if it sounds harsh, but that's reality. Bad things happen, but it's up to you to make things right.

12) *An ounce of perseverance is worth a pound of talent.* You're going to hear it over and over: "You can't, you can't, you can't; that's not possible; no, won't happen; you can't." Nonsense. I was told numerous times that I'd never be an officer while enlisted in the service, never go to flight school, never fly an advanced aircraft like the Blackhawk helicopter, never fly airplanes because the army only trains about 100 pilots per year, never get published, and on and on. I did all of those things! Forget about the

naysayers. Be persistent in your negotiations. Focus and you will prevail!

13) *Be nonchalant.* Yes, it's important to you to get your credit fixed, but don't get too exited or you'll make the person you are talking with nervous. You'll also tip your hand. Being nonchalant is the cornerstone of negotiating.

14) *Everything is negotiable.* This, of course, assumes that the person you're negotiating with is reasonable.

Just a few more thoughts on negotiating: reasonable people will always negotiate matters of dollars and "sense." If you find that you aren't making any headway when you're negotiating and someone is intransigent, then you're not likely dealing with a reasonable person. After all, we aren't talking about heirlooms here. You'll either need to a) change your tactics and/or b) change the players and/or c) go to a higher authority. You can also wait a while, and sometimes people change their minds—which is why it's important not to completely walk or burn bridges if it can be avoided.

But understand what you're dealing with. The types you will encounter will likely be both educated and uneducated derelicts; some of them may even be very intelligent. Notice that I didn't say smart. Intelligent people are those that can memorize things, perform well in school, and even understand sterile concepts that are complex. Being smart is something very different. Smart people are cunning, clever, or creative in a practical sense and use these qualities to achieve real world, desirable results. Reasonable people are often smart, and you need to be able to determine very quickly who is and who isn't reasonable so as not to waste too much time with front-line cronies with little common sense and even less sense of fair play and reason.

In the world of collection agencies and lawyers, you must prepare for the worst. I share this with you in an effort to prepare you for what will likely be very unpleasant, as discussions will invariably run afoul. Your preparation—achieving mental toughness—is a necessary element of credit repair, since collectors and lawyers have a penchant for abuse. They will make it personal, yell, and do everything they can to bait you into a verbal pissing contest.

Don't fall for it. You can't win this type of exchange, and it will do nothing to further your goals. Don't ever lose your cool, raise your voice, or say anything to stoop to that level. If you don't like what is being said, then say so clearly and succinctly, and then take it to a higher authority. Remember, harassment is illegal, but the law in and of itself is not a deterrent.

If your skin is thin, you'd better toughen it up and right now.

> **Tip:** When any stranger telephones you, always immediately ask for the caller's full name, company affiliation, location, and phone number. Say that you're in the middle of something right at the moment but you'll call him or her right back. This is not only a good practice to prevent harassment and promote safety, but it's also a good way to take notes on what collectors have called and when, and it puts them on a little different footing. Collectors are required to identify themselves, and if any collector fails to provide the information you ask for, then you know right then and there that: a) this isn't someone you can deal with on any level (after all, if he can't provide this simple bit of information, then how can you ever expect to negotiate with him on any issues that really matter?); b) you'll have a legal claim against him for failing to follow the FDCPA. (The next chapter, "Dealing with Collectors," will go into much more detail about this subject.) You do have Caller ID and Anonymous Caller Block, don't you? Caller ID can be used to determine who is who, and collectors wishing to call and harass are telling on themselves with Caller ID. Of course, if they do provide their information and then turn abusive, you'll have all of their information if you decide to take legal action against them.

Think very hard about the art of negotiation. Ponder it. Lose sleep over it. It's a very powerful thing and will serve you in your quest for clean credit and in many other endeavors in your life. Try it out on simple things like negotiating a price for a pair of slacks or anything else. You want to learn and polish this skill to the highest degree possible. Remember: *Nonchalance is the cornerstone of negotiating.*

The above discussion applies to creditors, not to CRAs. CRAs are to be treated with professional courtesy only, and when that fails the first time around, hammer them with letters containing legal jargon and threats of a lawsuit.

CRAs don't care about you. They are in business to make money, period. They make their money by selling information (names and addresses) to lenders. They lose money every time they talk with you, the consumer. Never forget it. However, sometimes they will not budge unless you have a lawyer send them a letter demanding what you want and threatening legal action if your demands are not met. Legal action is the last thing they want, and they have no interest in tangling with you over something they are really indifferent about. Actually, an actual lawsuit is what gets their attention; letters from lawyers are becoming less and less effective. I guess they figure most people don't have the kahunas to sue them when they screw up. I'm hoping you do; if enough people do it, then and only then will things change. In 2000, the three CRAs were fined $2.5 million by the Federal Trade Commission (FTC) for blocking millions of consumers from discussing the contents of their credit reports

### How to Approach Disputing Items on Your Report

Since one reporting agency may report different items than another, you must go to each CRA individually to handle problems with your credit report. For example, if you want to have a negative item removed, send a separate letter to each CRA concerning the specific item. You must track each letter you send by recording it in your log (in addition to using the insurance method—certified mail, return receipt requested).

Keeping notes on any written correspondence or actual conversations that follow will give you the ability to track what was said to and by whom as well as what was sent, received, and so on. These notes will come in very handy when you least expect it.

Never dispute more than two to three items at one time with a CRA, since it will likely raise red flags. Since you don't want them to know that you are using a credit repair technique, you should never do anything to raise suspicion. You can, however, dispute two or three items with one CRA while disputing two or three different items with another CRA.

As stated previously, keep in mind that your priority for attacking negative items may change depending upon where the item shows up. For example, if a negative item shows up on one report but not the other two, then you might consider moving that to a lower priority. However, if the item is very bad, you might make it a priority because some singular items are so bad (e.g., bad debts, judgments, repossessions) that they can, in and of themselves, prevent you from getting credit.

## How and When to Use a Lawyer

Hiring a lawyer to deal with your creditors and CRAs is a last resort. When the terms of written agreements aren't met, and when all other methods described have failed, then you should consider it very carefully and weigh your options. It's likely that you will know far more about credit than most lawyers when you are finished reading this book. Why pay someone to negotiate when you already know how?

In some cases, having a lawyer attempt to negotiate a settlement agreement when a lawsuit is imminent or send letters to CRAs when yours have failed can prove helpful. Just make sure that if you hire a lawyer, you know exactly what it is you want him or her to do and can explain *succinctly* what the strengths of your case are.

If you do decide to use a lawyer, don't look in the Yellow Pages. Go with someone who comes highly recommended by a friend or relative. If you can't get a friend to recommend an attorney, call the state bar association for a referral. Those on the referral list will often offer 30 to 60 minutes of consultation free of charge. In addition, the bar association will often have legal aid services available to people with meager means. The wait to get an appointment with one of these attorneys can be long in some cases, but you don't know if you don't ask.

I have known a good lawyer or two . . . it's difficult, but if you do find a good one treat him like gold.

Once, I was in the middle of a serious trademark dispute and, at the behest of a good friend of mine, I contacted an attorney he knew. He was so helpful in providing the documents that I needed. He even said, "You're a smart guy and you can figure this out." He provided me with the templates that I needed pro bono so that I could submit my own Answer to an Opposition that was filed by a very well-financed (and well-represented) company. The templates worked like a charm, and in the end I won a very sweet trademark.

Again, the attorney will likely not know as much as you do once you've read this book, but you can convey what you want to accomplish and he or she can write the letters or file suit.

Often lawyers are more willing to negotiate a deal when they feel confident that the defendant they are suing will pay them. If you hand them a case that is cut and dried, they will often take it on a contingency basis (i.e., they take their fee when and if they win). This fee can consist of attorney's fees that you've sued for and/or a portion of what you are awarded, usually one-third. An example would be a case against a collection agency that has called you outside allowable hours, for example, 7 A.M. This is a slam-dunk for an attorney, since all he or she has to do is subpoena the agency's phone records to prove it. Use your negotiating skills to convince the attorney that you have a winner. Take a copy of the FCRA and/or FDCPA with you and highlight the relevant portions so that you can wrap it all up in the first free consultation.

*Tip:* Sometimes you can get free legal assistance if you meet certain income requirements. Check with your state bar to find out more. Also, many law schools have legal clinics where students will do work pro bono. Law students are often looking for oddball cases, too, which is a category that credit often falls into. Go into these clinics with an open mind; maybe you can build a rapport with someone who will be the next Great American Lawyer.

If you can't get the attorney to take your case on contingency, I recommend that you get him or her to agree to a flat fee for each service provided, and get it in writing. If you can't get your lawyer to agree to these terms, find one who will.

In all of your written agreements with lawyers, use the phrase "This agreement constitutes the full work that attorney will conduct, and if there are any additional services to be performed, those services will be confirmed in writing and a price set separately in advance of the services."

Of course lawyers must get paid to earn a living, but it's up to you to protect yourself from overbilling and unscrupulous practices. After all, if you're overbilled and don't have anything in writing, what are you going to do? Unlike the rest of us, lawyers can represent themselves and forgo legal fees, creating an environment that's ripe for abuse. Where does that leave you?

**Note:** I've had written agreements with lawyers, only to have them go back on the deal and bill me for more than agreed. I've also had them agree to one thing over the phone, and then send me a contract that was different than what we agreed upon. And they're supposed to be working for me? In my opinion, they generally have earned their bad reputation. Don't take anything for granted, and be prepared to sue your lawyer and turn him or her into the state bar association if written agreements are broken.

## TAX CONSEQUENCES OF
## SETTLEMENTS AND CHARGE-OFFS

Let's face it—most great things come with a downside. Many people, even collectors, fail to realize this, but when a bank settles with a debtor or does a charge-off, the information is sent to the IRS via a Form 1099 for the year in which it occurred. Therefore, whatever you amount you don't pay the creditor will be treated as income. Thus, you will be taxed at whatever your rate was for that year. For example, if you make $25,000 at your job and have a standard deduction of $4,550, then you normally end up being taxed on $20,450. However, if you owed a bank or banks a total of $20,000 and only paid them $5,000, then your taxable income goes up to $35,450 ($20,450 plus the $15,000 you didn't pay).

What does this mean, exactly? Well, normally you would pay $3,071 in total tax, but since your taxable income went up by $15,000, you will owe $6,374. The difference is $3,303, and this is the amount the IRS is going to want from you when it discovers the charge-off. It often takes three years before things catch up to the IRS, but it could be sooner. If you get a 1099 from a bank you settled with, be sure to report the income. If it was for a previous year, simply file a form 1040X (amended return) and, if necessary, contact the IRS to schedule payment arrangements.

So what's the net difference of your settlement in this example? The bank forgave $15,000 but the IRS wants $3,303. Still not a bad deal at all.

## CREDIT REPORTING: HOW IT WORKS

How does information end up on your credit report? This is an area that can get very complicated and depends on many factors, such as what type of account it is, who the creditor is, whether or not the creditor is a member of a CRA, whether the creditor is affiliated with an association that is a member of the CRA, and whether or not the account has been turned over to a collection agency.

Mid- to large-size creditors have accounts with the CRAs and pay fees for the right to report. Smaller creditors can often open up accounts with the CRAs, paying a setup fee of around $300 and a monthly fee of $50, which enables them to report at will. (Equifax's business office claimed that it doesn't release exact guidelines for opening a business account and approves or denies applicants at its discretion. This seems dubious at best . . . Equifax is up to no good, and the policy surely can be challenged if someone chooses to pursue it.)

Equifax and Experian will not deal directly with landlords, so landlords must set up accounts with someone the CRA already does business with. In the case of Equifax, they do business with the National Association of Independent Landlords (NAIL), which in turn charges its clients $60 per month. In return, landlords can report information at will, simply by faxing their "universal data form" to Equifax. Experian does business with a couple of third-party companies—Landlord Protection Services and Allied Residence.

Trans Union will permit companies (and landlords) that will report at least 100 accounts per month to open a member account. It charges its clients a $305 setup fee and $95 annually to renew. It also does business with third-party vendors that report for other companies, including InterCept and The Service Bureau.

Non-landlords can set up a subscriber account with Experian that permits reporting, but the account holder must report 500 individuals per month. Experian also charges setup and membership fees.

Some of these CRAs are also unwilling to set up accounts with companies that are in certain lines of business. These include credit repair and debt consolidation firms, bail bond companies, and even lawyers that aren't in the sole business of collections. Experian has a program that enables smaller companies to report credit account information, but one full year of membership is required, and the companies must be in the business of extending credit to clients. There is a fee, of course, and there are also monthly minimums.

Since individuals and small businesses usually can't get something put on your credit report without being either a member of a CRA or a member of some sort of association that reports for the CRAs, they'll often turn to collection agencies and third parties—which do have accounts with CRAs and report diligently.

If this all seems complicated, I'll confound you further by relating a disheartening conversation with the third-party landlord reporting organization NAIL. It claimed that if it reports an item as delinquent and then a landlord later requests that the item be removed, it will not remove it. Allegedly NAIL can only report such an account as a 0 balance but not remove it. This is another case of the bully syndrome, and there's no justification for it. (Just one more situation that I believe could be successfully challenged in court should someone choose to pursue it.)

### Public Records

All public records are scanned by service bureaus—companies that work for the CRAs and provide data to them. This means that when you are being sued, have a judgment against you, have a lien against your property, or file for bankruptcy, it's likely to appear on your credit report. The problem is these service bureaus are careless, prone to make mistakes, and will often transcribe names, addresses, and Social Security numbers incorrectly.

### IN SUMMARY

- CRAs and creditors must never know or suspect that you are using a credit repair technique.
- Be nice to creditors and appeal to their emotions.
- Be courteous and professional to CRAs, but if that fails, get nasty.
- Treat each report as a separate issue.
- Never dispute more than two or three items at a time with a CRA, since it will raise a red flag.

- Lawyers are to be used as a last resort only.
- Keep in mind that there are tax consequences to settlements.
- Credit reporting can be performed by creditors using many methods, including third-party processors and collection agencies.

▲

# CHAPTER 4

# DEALING WITH COLLECTORS

One of the core elements of successful credit repair is your ability to deal with collectors, because they will be the ones who will be making many of the decisions on how they handle you and your account. Considering this, you will live and die by the way in which you handle "them." The information in this chapter is therefore among the most crucial in your quest to understand how to get what you want.

First of all, you need to know your rights. This will give you a fundamental understanding of what collectors and collection agencies can and cannot do. This understanding will provide the basis for the approach you will take and will further give you confidence so that you will not allow yourself to be intimidated. I refer to collectors and collection agencies separately because they differ in some of their procedures. Laws concerning how they must conduct themselves differ in some ways as well. Nevertheless, many of the basic rules regarding debt collections will apply to both.

## YOUR RIGHTS UNDER THE FDCPA

The Fair Debt Collection Practices Act (FDCPA) applies to personal, family, and household debts. This includes money owed on cars, medical care, or charge accounts. The FDCPA prohibits debt collectors from engaging in unfair, deceptive, or abusive practices while collecting these debts. The following are the rules under which collection agencies must operate:

- Debt collectors may contact you only between 8 A.M. and 9 P.M.
- Debt collectors may not contact you at work if they know your employer disapproves.
- Debt collectors may not harass, oppress, or abuse you.
- Debt collectors may not lie when collecting debts, such as falsely implying that you have committed a crime.
- Debt collectors must identify themselves to you on the phone.
- Debt collectors must stop contacting you if you ask them to stop in writing.
- Debt collectors may call your neighbors, but only to determine where you are, and only once. They may not discuss your debts.

In a nutshell, bill collectors from collection agencies cannot harass you by calling late, calling your neighbors repeatedly (or talking to them about your debts), calling your work, or at all! This means that you don't have to be a victim, and you can take action to see that the harassment stops or doesn't occur at all. There is a way to get collectors to stop contacting you, called a "cease communication" letter. This is explained in detail later in this chapter.

> **Note:** The Fair Debt Collection Practices Act (FDCPA) only applies to collection agencies. However, most creditors either don't know this or the ones that do abide by it anyway since they don't want to be sued. (That is, if the requests by the debtor for the creditor to perform something under this Act are written and sent certified mail returned receipt requested.)

The complete text of the Fair Debt Collection Practices Act can be found in Appendix D.

If collection agencies fail to abide by the rules, contact the FTC and the state attorney general where they reside immediately. You can also file suit if you are so inclined, depending on the situation. The best place to file such a lawsuit is in your state court, even if the collection agency is in another state. Jurisdiction will likely be determined by who called whom. If the collector called you, then you will sue in your state. Collection agencies can make motions to get the venue (location) changed and all sorts of other things to slow the process, but if they called you, then you have the right to sue them in your state. This is best, since you won't have to travel to their state to appear at pretrial hearings and such.

As a bill collector, I witnessed abuse of biblical proportions, and few debtors did anything about it. Collectors will likely abuse you if you let them, so make sure that you are clear on the front end that you won't stand for any of that.

Even the ones who don't abuse you will lie about the rules. The worst abusers are the ones from collection agencies. But don't be alarmed; there are ways of dealing with them and ridding yourself of them for good. Creditors' collectors typically lie as well, but not to the same extent. Overall, the cruelty of these unsavory characters is without equal. Even very minor infractions by very good customers (e.g., a payment that's one month late) will often yield the most poisonous venom that can be spoken from human lips. It's all smiles until you miss a payment, regardless of the circumstance, then it's no-holds-barred abuse.

Once, I missed a single payment after having a perfect record for 11 years with a major bank. The check was returned by the post office for failure to provide postage, which of course can happen to anyone. When I provided the returned envelope with the postmark to the creditor and explained the circumstances (it was even stamped with the USPS "returned for postage"), all I got was abuse and indifference. (Even worse, I was not even dealing with the collection department of the creditor, but customer service!) Sadly, this is the rule rather than the exception. Believe me when I tell you that even if you were to lose all of your limbs serving your country, they would still treat you like dirt.

> **Note:** Collectors will not heed your verbal warnings and will continue to break the rules, since a) few people actually sue, and b) the penalty is so small—maximum of $1,000 per occurrence in most states—that it's not enough of a deterrent. The FTC will go after collection agencies with enough complaints filed against them, which is why it's important that you report every violation to the FTC and to your state's attorney general. (The FTC, for example, has gone after collection agency Performance Capital Management, Inc., of Irvine, California, with a proposed fine of $2 million.)

### Record Phone Conversations

You might consider recording phone conversations with collectors using a small mini-cassette recorder (~$25) and telephone listening adapter (~$5) from Radio Shack. But be advised, in some states you must inform the other party that you are recording the conversation and the person must agree to being recorded. (In many states, only one party has to know that recording is taking place; however, just because something is legal doesn't make it admissible in court. Check your state laws before recording.) If you feel that you must record and the person won't agree, simply tell him or her that you're sorry, but you won't discuss the matter until you are permitted to tape the conversation. Be polite but firm.

Recording phone conversations can go a long way toward making sure that you aren't mistreated. When recording, be certain to say the date and the name of the person you are speaking with and which collection agency he or she represents. This kind of evidence will also go a long way in court (in some states) should you decide to sue. The downside to this tactic is that it often puts the person you're speaking with on the defensive. You may want to use this technique only after a conversation has gone badly and you have been abused.

Note that this is primarily a technique for dealing with collection agencies, not for collectors in general. (A collector is usually a third party operating on behalf of the creditor. Creditors will also have in-house collectors, who can be quite nasty, but often not to the same extent.) Never be afraid to record conversations with agencies, since they are the most likely to be abusive.

As you will learn upon further reading, you don't need collection agencies and can often take them out of the loop entirely. One exception to this is if the agency has purchased the debt from the original creditor, in which case you may or may not need the agency, depending on a) what you are willing to put up with, b) if the amount is so small that legal action isn't a concern, c) what the agency can or can't take from you, and so on. Personally, if an agency was abusive and they didn't own the debt, I'd tell them to stick it and then send a cease communication letter, as described in detail below, under "Take the Collection Agency out of the Loop." (See Appendix A for an example.)

It's best to contact collectors on your terms, and the next section explains how to go about this. Once you have contact with them, if they are rude, politely let them know that you fully understand the FDCPA and expect them to abide by the rules. As you begin discussions with them and they get nasty, tell them that you are willing to discuss your accounts in a professional manner, but if they break the rules, you will not only notify the FTC and the state attorney general, but you will sue them for any violations. Will they take you seriously? Probably not; they will likely continue on their course until you take legal action. The only thing they understand is the hammer. They really don't want to be sued, since the legal fees for defense will cost them money. Yet they won't believe you'll sue until you actually do it.

## GET LOST

Now that you understand your rights, you have to decide how you will deal with contacting particular collectors or agencies. It is always best to do so on your terms. What I mean by this is, are you running? Do they know where you are now? Can you move? Did you move already? Is your phone number listed or unlisted? Do you want them to have your phone number?

I take the cautious approach. That is, if I'm lost I stay that way. If I'm not lost I get lost. Why? Because most collectors are scum, and they will make your life hell without regard to the rules, even if you make it clear that you know the rules. In many cases you must be prepared to sue when dealing with them, so keep very good records of whom you spoke with, when, who called whom, and what was said.

The cautious approach is one where the collector doesn't know where you are and doesn't know your number.

### Privacy in the Information Age

The following methods will not only assist you in dealing with collectors on your terms, they will also serve to protect you from unwanted intrusions, which can take many forms. These, combined with identity theft prevention techniques (covered in Chapter 9), are also good for your overall safety and sanity:

- When you move, don't file a change of address form with the post office, or if you must, list a P.O. Box.
- Get an unlisted phone number. If you can, get rid of your landline and use a prepaid cellular phone.
- When you call any collector, be sure to use Caller ID Block (start your call by dialing *67) so they can't get your number. Understand that if you are calling an 800 number, Caller ID Block doesn't work. In this case, you might want to get the collector's local number with area code (this may be printed on a collection letter you've received, or you can try information by dialing the area code + 555-1212. To get the area code, look in the front of any phone book for nationwide are code table or log onto www.intrepidsoft.com/acjava.html and use the site's area code utility.
- Get "anonymous caller blocking" (available from any phone company). Many collectors use a Caller ID blocker so that their number does not show up on the Caller ID box of the person they are calling. Anonymous caller blocking is a countermeasure that prevents all callers to your number from using Caller ID blocker.
- When you send mail to collectors, don't use a return address on the envelope.
- When you have utilities installed, use an alias first name (middle name works as a substitute) and password protect the accounts.
- Password protect all other accounts so that someone who obtains your Social Security number (collectors have that) can't pose as you and get your address, phone number, or other information from other creditors and various third parties.
- Give your relatives a cellular phone number if you can, and inform them that they are not to give out your number to anyone.
- If you have e-mail and want to use it to negotiate with collectors, don't give out an e-mail address that is traceable or a Web-based address. That is, if it's harry@microsoft.com, the collector will know that you work for Microsoft. If it's

another Web-based e-mail address, all the collector has to do is check to see who owns the domain name and he's found you. Use Hotmail or another generic e-mail account.

- Never sign for anything that's sent to you via certified mail, return receipt requested. If you have roommates, make sure they know that they are not to sign for anything that is addressed to you.
- Assume that a collector can get your phone number in spite of your precautions. Screen your phone calls using Caller ID and an answering system. If your Caller ID does not identify the caller, have the answering machine pick the call up. Use a generic message on your machine, such as, "I'm not in; please leave a message." Do not use your name.

*Tip:* Consider also that your address is given to CRAs by creditors. So if you have accounts that are in good standing and want those good-standing creditors to have your address, give them a P.O. Box. Otherwise, you will have collectors calling your neighbors and telling them all about what you owe and to whom. Further, if you are applying for credit and wish to avoid using a P.O. Box since it might hurt your chances of being approved, consider providing the address of a relative or a close friend. When you apply for credit, the address you give the lender will be provided to the CRAs. It's the world we live in, right or wrong.

Does this seem like a lot of trouble to go through? Maybe, but if you've ever dealt with collectors, you'll understand why it's necessary.

In some cases you can't move or disappear because you have a house or because of other circumstances. In this case, you can use any variation of the methods I describe in order to mitigate the problem.

*Tip:* Don't confuse getting lost with running. Always keep in mind that collectors hate debtors that run and

*those with whom they have trouble establishing com-
munications. So contact them on a regular basis and
just explain that you don't have a phone.*

## NEGOTIATING A SETTLEMENT

Once you contact the collector or collection agency on
your terms, politely make it clear that you understand the
rules. Once you have established some ground rules, you can
begin negotiating, and you must take a conciliatory approach.
Remember, you are negotiating a settlement, and you have to
get the person to come around to your way of thinking. When
you have any item that has gone past 90 days late, it goes into
collections. In collections, the average collection rate is 15 to
20 percent of the total debt. Since creditors know this, they
will do everything they can to settle the debt at this crucial
point. They will try to collect for about 90 more days, and if
they are unsuccessful, they will turn the debt over to a collection agency. They really don't want this, since their chances
of collecting at this point is very small, and whatever is collected must by shared with the agency; often 50 percent will
go to the collector. Your chances of negotiating a good settlement just before it goes to an agency are quite good, but don't
be alarmed if you can't settle before this happens.

Don't get personal, and don't argue. Simply state the facts
and don't allow yourself to be abused on any level. Avoid ultimatums whenever possible when dealing with all collectors,
especially in-house collectors for creditors. In the case of
unruly collection agencies, have the matter referred back to
the original creditor (see "Take the Collection Agency out of
the Loop," below).

*Tip: Often a collector will try to get you to send any
money at all, which will make the seven-year clock for
the negative account start all over. Yes, most negative
credit remains on your report for seven years, as
described in an earlier chapter. But the seven-year*

*clock begins from the date of last activity; sending money is activity. You may have a debt that is six years old that you haven't paid. Normally it would drop off in one more year; yet paying anything at all will make it seven more years. Don't send a dime until you have an agreement in writing!*

When negotiating, be sure to tell the truth and stay real. Don't insult anyone or belittle them (even if they are stupid). Don't take a deal you don't want or cannot live up to. Remember to just hang in there. Collectors will keep trying to beat you down, but you will beat them down! Remember to review "The Art of Negotiation" in Chapter 3.

Collection agencies are in the business of collecting money, period. It's what they do, and they are good at it, which is why they are in business and creditors use them. Collectors from these organizations are even more abusive and loathsome (yes, I worked for a collection agency, &^%*!). The agency doesn't get any money if it doesn't collect, and the collector doesn't have a job long if he or she doesn't collect money. This is quite a motivator, and so collectors will do anything in order to collect, including lying, cheating, badgering, and so on.

> **Note:** An agency will get a commission for the money it collects, from 30 to 50 percent on average. This is one reason it's often easier to settle with a creditor before the account goes to an outside agency, since the creditor knows it costs money to collect using an agency.

Debts are categorized into mainly two categories: secured and unsecured. If the debt you owe is secured, this makes your job more difficult, because the creditor can simply come and take the collateral away using the courts if the terms and conditions loan aren't met. However, banks are not in the real estate or auto business; they just loan money and want it back plus their interest. You can sometimes renegotiate the terms even on secured debt if the bank feels it is cheaper than taking legal action against you. Make sure that when you renegotiate the terms, you get it in writing, and make sure that the terms include removal of any negative history on your credit report.

With unsecured debts, it's much easier to negotiate a settlement. There isn't anything that the creditor can come and take, so you are in a very good position. Even if all negotiations fail, it's often unlikely that they will ever collect, even if they get a judgment, unless you own a home or car that the creditor can put a lien on. A lien is an expensive proposition for a creditor due to the legal costs involved, so it's not often used with smaller debts. The creditor must be fairly certain of the odds of collecting in order to take such steps. If you are on the phone negotiating with a creditor, such a step is unlikely, even if it is threatened. There are no hard-and-fast rules as to what an individual creditor will and will not do, and you should judge every threat on its own merits.

Often collectors will say that credit history cannot be changed. Simply inform them that you know that they are mistaken and that you are willing to make a deal, but it's up to them to remove the derogatory history as part of any settlement. Don't make ultimatums. Keep the dialogue open for as long as it serves to make progress toward your goals. If you aren't getting anywhere, have the matter referred back to the creditor (in the case of a collection agency), or go higher up the food chain if it's the creditor you're dealing with. As a matter of settlement, any negative item can be changed or deleted altogether.

> ***Tip***: *Never tell on yourself. For example, creditors will often want you to fill out forms that list your income and obligations (financial statement). Don't do it. Why supply ammunition? Further, if you are disabled and collecting Social Security, you must decide whether or not to admit it (if asked). There's no harm in a little white lie; it's none of their business anyway. (They*

*shouldn't be asking such questions. There's nothing in your contract with them that says you consented to a rectal exam.) Don't tell them anything that will hinder your negotiations for debt reduction. You can play the pauper; this is always believable, since few people have money. Or you can say that you have many more obligations than just what you owe them. Just remember, don't ever tell a white lie that you will get caught in, and be sure to take copious notes of discussions with creditors and review them before each conversation. Steer clear of flat-out lies; only white lies are acceptable in my opinion, even if the collector happens to be a scumbag. White lies are simply untrue answers to questions that should not be asked in the first place, or niceties that are said in order to spare someone's feelings.*

## TAKE THE COLLECTION AGENCY OUT OF THE LOOP

Collection agencies are notorious for being very wicked and demanding all of the money at once without delay. But you have the collection agency by the kahunas. If your negotiations are getting nowhere (and the agency won't accept a restrictively endorsed check, as described in Chapter 8, you can send a "cease communication" letter. (See Appendix A for an example.) In effect, if you request that the agency no longer contact you, it must refer the matter back to the original creditor. You can stipulate in the letter that the agency has one more chance to settle (e.g., within 10 days), spelling out the exact terms, but that if your terms are not accepted you no longer wish to be contacted. This can work in your favor in one of two ways: either the agency will wish to settle in order to get paid, or, if the account does go back to the creditor then the creditor will be more likely to negotiate with you. But be advised, the creditor can sue if it appears that there is any money in doing so.

**Note:** Usually creditors will not talk to you about an account while it's still in the hands of an agency. But if they do, and you've agreed to settle with the original creditor while the matter is still in the hands of the agency, make sure that you word any agreement in such a manner as to include not only the stipulation that a) all credit reporting agencies be notified to "remove any derogatory reference" and b) "the relevant collection agency" also be notified to delete the marks from its database and stop reporting the debt to the CRAs. The collection agency is required to report the debt as indicated by the creditor, unless you are disputing the account and prove otherwise.

It's likely that you will have far more success dealing with the original creditor than a collection agency. So when an account is handed over to a collection agency, your best bet is to try once for a good settlement and then have the matter referred back to the original creditor.

> **Tip:** If your account has gone to a third-party collection agency and they haven't purchased the debt (i.e., they are collecting on behalf of the creditor), sending the agency a cease communication letter and getting the debt referred back to the creditor can also be good for your credit. Collection agencies report bad credit with far more regularity, and often create new account numbers for the same account so as to compound your report with even more problems. Keep your negotiating with them restricted to days, not weeks. If you send a cease communication letter and get the matter referred back quickly enough, you can possibly avoid a further tattering of your report.

### Debts that Get Sold to Third Parties

Many creditors will sell debts after 180 days have elapsed. Although they will perform a charge-off, thereby providing some tax relief, they often will sell the debt to third parties. These third parties are companies that believe they can collect more money from a debtor than the price they paid to acquire the debt. This price varies but can typically range from 5 to 15 percent of the debt.

This situation often creates significant problems for you in your attempts at bad credit removal. You're still in a good position for a reduced settlement, but removing the bad marks from your credit report can be much more difficult. This is due to that fact that the original creditor has sold the debt and thus no longer has a motivation to remove the bad history. The company that purchased the debt, on the other hand, has no control over what the original creditor reports. Furthermore, and far more insidious, is a propensity for the current owner of the debt to report the account as a collection account under its company name (and a different account number). When this happens, the same account will often show up as two different ones on your report. Fair? I don't think so.

Even more troublesome is the possibility of the third-party buyer's obtaining a judgment against you. Usually third-party buyers will do this after 90 days of attempting to settle the account, so often you can negotiate a good settlement before this happens. Just remember that the settlement agreement must state that the third party will remove derogatory credit history that it is reporting.

If a judgment is obtained, there are still some options for getting this information taken off your report (more on this in Chapter 7). Keep in mind that judgments will remain on your report for 10 years (and are renewable for 10 more years in some states), so it is important that you avoid them if possible. This still doesn't solve the problem of the original creditor, however. But after a few years, the original creditor may be willing to remove the bad history under some conditions, such as when you have a new account with them—perhaps a secured account—that is in good standing. Often people change jobs, and you may find someone more agreeable in the credit reporting department who wasn't there when you were attempting to negotiate before.

Since it is to your benefit for the original creditor to retain a debt (rather than selling it to a third party), it's important that you try to find out as much information as you can about your creditor's intentions. Of course, the original creditor can get a judgment, but this doesn't present the many hurdles associated with the debt's being sold to a third party. (It's one item, with one party to deal with, and you still have the leverage of the money you owe.) If you can, find out what the creditor does with debts after they charge them off. Often the creditor will tell you, and keep in mind that what one person won't reveal, another person will. If charged-off accounts are turned over to third-party buyers, this can affect your tactics for settlement and negotiation. To every extent possible, you want to avoid a debt's being sold, even if it means paying more than you thought or settling for terms that are somewhat less desirable.

## COLLECTION LAWYERS

There are two types of lawyers that will attempt to collect debts—in-house lawyers and those that are contracted. In-house lawyers are usually employees of the creditor or collection agency. The ones that are contracted don't often work for the creditor, but they have other clients as well. In collection matters, often contract lawyers will not get paid unless they collect money, but the in-house lawyers will usually get paid a salary.

Large banks usually have in-house attorneys, while smaller credit unions often do not. Of course, an attorney representing a doctor with a small practice will likely be a contract attorney. The size of the organization will often dictate what type of lawyer they have.

Regardless of which kind of lawyer you come across, they all have the same basic criteria for deciding whether or not to sue. It comes down to one thing: if there's money in it for them and their clients (in the case of contract lawyers) or the creditor they work for (in the case of in-house lawyers), they will sue.

A lawyer will assess the situation based on how much is owed and what he or she can take. It's just that simple. If you have wages to garnish or assets to seize, and the amount is worth the trouble, then you are likely to be sued. However, settling is always preferable to suing, since litigation costs money and there's always a chance that the creditor will get a judgment but still never collect. Debtors frequently have numerous obligations, and creditors that have obtained judgments have to wait in line behind other creditors with a priority (e.g., the IRS or a mortgage lender). If creditors sense that they may have to "take a number," then this will impact their decision about suing.

Keep in mind that this rule is not hard and fast, since people generally make bad decisions no matter what their education and intelligence quotient. In fact, some lawyers and creditors are downright stupid, and I've seen them make bad decisions with regularity. This is why you have to bring them around to a more prudent line of thinking, primarily using your negotiation skills.

If a creditor's attorney is handling your case, as with all negotiations, be nice. Explain that you wish to do the best you can to resolve the issue—just like you would say to any other creditor. Don't panic by racing out and retaining a lawyer to represent you. That will not be necessary if you play your cards right. However, if litigation is imminent and you get a notice to appear in court, by all means get a lawyer without delay. Often you can still settle before the court date if you have a lawyer in your corner, particularly since your obtaining a lawyer means that the creditor will likely have to spend more money in its litigation. Your lawyer, if he is worth his salt, will create myriad hurdles for the opposition—which can get costly for them.

You have to assume that the opposing lawyer has done some research on you, attempting to find out your place of employment, salary, assets, and obligations. The lawyer may have some or all of the facts, and you must try and discover what has been uncovered if possible by letting him or her speak. (Remember the section on the art of negotiation, and review it often.)

Don't tell on yourself. If you make a good salary and have money to burn, why supply the motivation to sue you by saying so? Stick to the facts about the debt, and explain that times could be better. (This is not a lie, as times can always be better, right?) You want to make the attorney think that there is nothing to be gained from suing and it is in everyone's best interest to settle. If the lawyer and creditor believe it's more cost effective to settle, then they will. As always, appeal to the better part of their nature.

## JUST CONSIDER

- You have rights.
- Don't be abused.
- Negotiate on your terms.
- Be polite.
- Record when necessary.
- Get lost if necessary, but stay in contact on your terms.
- Take the collection agency out of the loop if necessary.
- Review "The Art of Negotiation."
- The obstacles will be the people. It's up to you to persevere.
- You don't have to give your phone number.
- You don't have to talk about your other debts or income.
- Ask for what you want in pieces. Save the credit report stuff for last if you are looking to reduce your debt.
- Take your time. You don't have to make a deal that day. In fact, walking away and coming back with a compromise is often best. Wait at least two days.
- Don't be intimidated by lawyers. They put their pants on one leg at a time, don't they?
- As much as possible, avoid allowing debts to get sold to third parties.
- Consider suing if you have been wronged.

▲

# CHAPTER 5

# THINGS YOU CAN DO RIGHT NOW TO IMPROVE YOUR SCORE

There are some easy things you can do immediately to improve your score, not least of which is to *begin now and forevermore to pay your bills on time.* You'd be surprised how rapidly things improve once you do this one thing.

In addition, you can do three additional things: make sure positive information gets reported, reestablish years of good credit where none existed before, and remove negative information that you know to be false.

## MAKE SURE POSITIVE INFORMATION GETS REPORTED

Got a college loan with a perfect payment history that isn't on one of the reports? Perhaps you have an old credit card or installment loan that didn't make it on the reports.

Items that are in good standing often go unreported, and it's up to you to make sure they get on your report. Since many lenders use credit scoring, the good stuff can boost your score, and you should make every effort to contact the creditors with whom you have a good payment history and see that they report it to the CRAs.

If you have evidence of such accounts, contact the CRAs yourself. Once again, use the insurance method. Write down everything—whom you spoke with and when—and then follow up. If you don't have evidence of such accounts, simply contact the creditors, and they'll usually be more than happy to provide you with a letter (get a copy for yourself *and* have them send a copy directly to the CRAs). To be certain that it gets reported, you should send a copy of the creditor's letter to each of the CRAs. In addition, ask the creditor to begin reporting the positive account to the CRAs.

## REESTABLISH CREDIT

You can start your road to recovery right away by placing as much distance as possible between you and your bad credit. This means:

- Always pay your bills on time, without exception.
- Open some secured credit card accounts. A secured card is one that requires a deposit at a bank. Your credit limit is usually the amount of the deposit but can be less or more. These cards are very easy to open, even with bad credit. You can also get a debit card, which basically takes any purchase right out of your checking account, making the balance in the account your limit.
- Convert these cards to unsecured accounts when possible, usually one year after opening, provided there hasn't been any negative payment history during that year.
- Make sure that you have both a savings and checking

account and use the checking account to pay your bills. Never, ever write a bad check.

- CDs (certificates of deposit) are a good way to establish rapport with a bank. Open one up (the minimum CD is usually $1,000 with a six-month term, which means that you can't take the money out before the term is up or you'll pay a penalty). After a while, you can borrow on that CD with the bank you opened it with; that is, obtain a loan using the CD as security against it. Make the payments on time without fail.

- If possible, obtain unsecured cards as well. Sometimes this requires the help of a cosigner, which can be a friend or family member with good credit. If they balk at the idea, tell them that you're just reestablishing credit and this will often help.

- Stay put! If you can avoid it, don't move or change jobs. This affects your ability to get credit, particularly if you have bad credit already.

*Tip: For many different reasons, those with a check-ered credit past—even those with a lot of money—often drop out of the credit reporting system altogether, opt-ing instead to use cash to pay for everything. Even if you have a bad credit history, this is the last thing you want to do; it just makes things worse. It's something people inevitably regret, since credit approval involves not only good credit but recent credit. Keep two or three accounts open and in good standing, and, if possible, mix up the types of accounts, e.g., one or two credit cards and one installment loan (for a car, for example).*

## ESTABLISH YEARS OF GOOD CREDIT
## WHERE NONE EXISTED BEFORE

This little-known secret absolutely takes the cake. I love this technique. It's so simple and powerful, yet hardly anyone knows about it!

1. Locate a friend or family member with a Visa or MasterCard that is in perfect standing.
2. Convince him or her to assign you as a secondary cardholder. (You might do so by agreeing to turn over the card once it comes in the mail so you will never use it. Or use whatever means of negotiating a deal that you think will be most effective.)
3. Once you've sealed the deal, get a copy of the person's credit report and make sure the account is in good standing. This may seem presumptuous, but a) if they're willing to do such a thing then you're already darn familiar anyway, and b) you can't risk adding negative credit to your own.
4. Once you're satisfied that the account is in good standing, have the person send a letter to the card issuer requesting that you be added to the account as a secondary cardholder and stating in writing that he or she will take responsibility for paying the balance.
5. The new card should arrive within a few weeks, or you may just receive an application or request for additional information. Either way, it is usually sent to the primary cardholder. If an application is required, you will fill out the coapplicant part. The card should arrive soon!
6. Wait 90 days and then order a copy of your report. It should show the credit card in good standing, open for as long as the original primary cardholder had it! Nuts!

**Note:** Keep in mind also that if the primary cardholder becomes delinquent, the negative history shows up on your report! In addition, balances can negatively affect your score; if large balances are carried, this can be harmful.

## REMOVE INFORMATION THAT IS NEGATIVE BUT FALSE

You may have items on your report that are outright false that can be settled very quickly. For instance:

- *The item isn't yours and never was.* Maybe a debtor has the same name as you, and his mistake ended up on your report. Simply contact the creditor in writing and explain that the Social Security numbers or previous or current addresses (or whatever) don't match. Have the creditor issue a letter to you and to all three CRAs explaining the mistake. Remember, *get the name of the person with whom you spoke and write it down!* Have the creditor fax the letter to you if possible, and then provide it to the CRAs yourself via certified mail, return receipt requested. Again, this is known as the "insurance method." In all things relating to credit repair, never assume anything.

- *The item was paid on time but shows paid late.* In many cases it's just a mistake. (They do happen, you know!) Contact the creditor and explain the situation. Often the creditor will agree that it was a mistake and correct it. Again, use the insurance method. Get the name of the person you spoke with, and have him or her send (fax is best) a copy of the correction to you and to the CRAs. As a backup, you should send the correction to the CRAs as well, via certified mail, return receipt requested.

If the creditor won't help, try getting the CRAs to remove the item. You may have enough proof (e.g., a canceled check or receipt of payment) in your possession to get it removed on your own. Depending on the situation, this may even be your first course of action! If I had irrefutable proof of payment, then I might just send the proof to the CRAs and skip the creditor altogether.

> **Caution:** If you don't have proof and need the creditor to provide you with it, don't reveal the fact that you've lost your receipt. This could open up Pandora's Box if the creditor has the scruples of Enron executives. Simply ask that the creditor provide a letter to the CRAs as described above and send you a copy.

If either the creditor or the CRAs fail to respond favorably even after you've requested help nicely, ask to speak to the manager. Continue moving up the chain of command with your request until you believe you've exhausted your efforts. If your short-term efforts fail, make sure you initiate further correspondence in writing and send it by certified mail, requesting a return receipt.

If things get bad enough down the road, you may have to threaten to get an attorney and sue for damages. I assure you, creditors—and sometimes the CRAs at this point—will often deny any knowledge of your previous contact. Be nice nonetheless, and explain in your "last ditch effort" written correspondence that they'll be hearing from your attorney if they don't do the right thing. There's plenty of time for your attorney to get nasty later. Be sure to review the section on how and when to use a lawyer.

Recently I read an article in *USA Today* about a lawsuit, Case No. 02CC15162, involving Washington Mutual bank.

In late 2002, the Alonsos experienced a number of unforeseen difficulties and fell behind in their loan payments. They received a default notice, but in July 2002 entered into a repayment agreement with the bank by which they would make monthly payments in the amount of $3,994.89, beginning in August 2002. On August 30, 2002, Mrs. Alonso went in person to Washington Mutual to make the first payment, but did not have a copy of the repayment agreement with her. She asked a teller to look up her home loan account and was told that the amount due was $3,943.33. Relying on that information, she wrote a check for that amount.

On September 10th, the Alonsos received a letter from Washington Mutual, returning their check and informing them that, as partial payments were not acceptable, the loan was immediately in foreclosure. Their efforts to pay the remaining $51.56 fell through, as they were never able to connect with the bank's designated officer, even though repeated attempts were made. Washington Mutual informed plaintiffs that if they did not enter into a modification of their repayment plan, they would foreclose on the house on September 24, 2002. To their complete shock, the Alonsos learned that their home sold at foreclosure on September 20, 2002.

Apparently, there are class actions being brought against Washington Mutual as well, and, if the allegations are true, it appears that this bank has been failing to post payments made by hundreds of consumers.

The lesson is, *bad things can happen to good people at the hands of a trusted institution.* Erroneous billing is quite common, and it's usually followed by collection action, so always keep your receipts of payment, and as soon as something begins to run amuck, you'd better take good notes. (Carefully read Chapter 7: Court—A Useful and Viable Option.)

▲

# CHAPTER 6

# REMOVING INFORMATION THAT IS NEGATIVE BUT TRUE

This is the chapter that is of the most interest to people, because it is the negative but true information that can usually take the most time and effort to fix. Also, there are many different scenarios around which negative credit can exist, such as:

- Is it a repossession or simply a late payment situation?
- Is money owed?
- Is money not owed?
- How much is owed?
- Who is owed . . . a bank, a doctor?
- Is it secured (collateral used, like a house or car) or unsecured debt?
- How long has it been owed?
- When was the last time a payment was made?
- How often were you late?
- Is the account open or is it closed?

- Is legal action of some kind expected, or has it occurred?
- Do you have wages that can be garnished or property that can be seized?

All of these questions must be answered so that the proper course of action can be determined. Look at each item that is negative and take notes, answering all of the questions above. Once you have all of the answers, you can begin to pursue the remedy.

First, look at the age of the debt. By law, negative credit shows on a report for seven years from the last transaction. That means seven years from the last time you made a payment. If the debt is old enough and will fall off of your credit report relatively soon (or soon enough for your needs), you cannot even waste your time with it; put it at the bottom of your priority list.

> **Warning:** Often collectors will try to get you to make a payment of any kind, even a tiny one of $10 or $20. Don't fall for it! If you make that payment, the seven-year clock starts all over again! Ouch!

Once you know the age of the debt and have determined that it's worthwhile to pursue, look at whether or not money is owed. If it is owed, then you have some bargaining power. You can use this power in negotiations, since creditors just want their money. If you don't owe money, this will affect your position when negotiating, and you will have to appeal even more to emotions.

Is the debt secured or unsecured? Again, secured debt requires you to put up collateral for the money, such as a car or home. Unsecured debt is backed up only by your promise to pay and doesn't require any collateral at all. Why is this important in removing negative credit? With unsecured debt such as credit card balances, you are in a much better position to negotiate, since the creditor has no power, other than to ruin your credit or get a judgment. Ruining your credit doesn't get creditors their money back, nor does obtaining a judgment against you guarantee they will. Just because a creditor gets a judgment against you doesn't mean they will ever collect. There must be assets to take, such as a house, car, or bank account, or wages to garnish. (We will go into judgments in further detail in a later section.)

> **Note:** There is pending legislation in Congress, H.R. Fair Credit Reporting Act Amendments of 2001. This act, which is expected to pass, will mandate that items that have been placed for collection or charged off must be removed from the credit report after three years, but only if certain conditions are met. The caveats are that a) such removal can only be performed one time per consumer, b) the debt cannot be greater than $100, and c) the consumer (debtor) must have attended a credit and financial management class during the three-year period. (It's still unclear what qualifies as a credit and financial management class, but this will likely be cleared up when the final legislation is passed.)

Few attempts will be made to get a judgment on unsecured debt unless there is considerable money owed. It costs creditors money to get a judgment, and they will only get one if they think it can help them get their money back. There is no hard-and-fast rule, but considering legal fees, it's unlikely that an attempt for a judgment will be made for unsecured debt of less than $1,200. Even for higher amounts it may not be attempted if the creditor does not ever expect to collect. An example of this would be a debt of $15,000 where it is well documented that the debtor is disabled and will likely never be able to pay. Why spend money on legal fees if the likelihood is that the money is wasted? Creditors don't want to get even; they just want their money. If you are not working and haven't worked, then clearly the creditor can't garnish income that isn't there. If, in addition to the lack of income, there are no assets to seize, then litigation is even less likely. Always keep in mind, many third-party companies that have purchased your debt have a system, and it doesn't matter what the circumstances are concerning your individual debt. Their cookie-cutter approach is to acquire debt at pennies on the dollar, attempt to collect for 90 days, and then obtain a judgment.

> **Note:** Social Security income, VA pensions, pension benefits, unemployment benefits, welfare, and child support (to the extent it is actually needed for basic living expenses) are exempt from garnishment.

To whom is the money owed? This affects your chances at removal. If it's owed to a single person such as a doctor, then it's often easier to negotiate with him than a large bank, since you know exactly where the buck stops and the doctor just wants his or her money. If it's owed to a department store, you're likely to encounter a certain amount of flexibility, since the store wants your business and the debt is unsecured. If it's owed to a credit card company, the chances are good that you can negotiate a settlement and get the item removed. A mortgage with a bank can be more difficult if you don't have any other source of leverage other than your house payment. A car loan? The creditor can always repossess the car if they haven't already. All creditors, however, will deal if there is something in it for them.

How often were you late? Was it patterned lateness or scattered? If patterned (adjacent in time), then your chances are better, since it can be demonstrated that the lateness occurred during a particular rough period, for example, you lost your job, got a divorce, and so on. If scattered, then it appears to the creditor that you are a little flaky or unreliable in general. (They are always assessing you, sizing you up: Can you be trusted? Can they make money from you in the future? How much can they get away with without ruining their cozy situation of charging you exorbitant interest on your open accounts?)

How long ago were you late? If it's been more than two years, your chances are better at removal. In the case of more recent account lateness, then it's a little bit harder. If the debt is older, you can use it in your negotiations . . . so and so happened during that time . . . blah, blah, blah.

Is the account still open? If so, the creditor is making money off of you and will continue to want to do so. The creditor will do what it takes to keep you as a customer because you are profitable.

> **Tip:** Since the credit report will show who closed an account, the lender or the consumer, it looks better if you closed it. If you know that you are going to become late on an open account, close it. Revolving accounts can be closed even if there's an outstanding balance. (Close accounts in writing only, using certified mail, return receipt requested. I'm currently suing a creditor for falsely reporting "account closed by credit grantor." Of course, I have the name/date/time/operator number of the person I spoke with when I closed it. If the creditor closed the account, as part of a settlement agreement you may want them to change the report to show that you closed it. Not critical, but something else to go for.

> **Tip:** In addition to getting derogatory credit removed and having the record of who closed the account changed, also consider getting the creditor to remove the inquiries. Often, when debts are in collections, creditors will inquire repeatedly on your report. This greatly hampers your ability to get credit. Remember, however, to look at the whole picture. If you are getting 75 percent off of a debt and bad credit removed as well, don't get hung up on this detail. On the other hand, if you are paying 100 percent of a debt, by all means get the inquiries off. The important thing is the bad mark; everything else is secondary. Inquiries will only stay on your report for two years. Just don't get greedy, since you

*could lose your credibility and the whole thing will blow up in your face. After you have a deal with the creditor, you can always go back later and often get the CRA to remove the inquiry, as prescribed in the removing inquiries section. Think about your options and your methods, while using a methodical approach.*

## ANALYZE YOUR SITUATION BEFORE YOU ACT

In the final analysis, it pays to look at your situation from a holistic perspective. Of course individual debts must be looked at for their unique circumstance, but once that is accomplished you should look at the entire situation. In a case where money is owed to many different creditors, you must determine these two things: Do you have the money to settle with all of your creditors? If so, will those creditors remove the derogatory history?

Obviously, the second question cannot be answered until you've spoken with all of your creditors. Go fishing first; see what they will agree to. Once you know what they are all willing to do, it's far easier to decide whom to pay, how much, and whether or not to pay any of them at all. If your situation is such that five of seven creditors agree to your terms, with the other two on the brink of obtaining a judgment, perhaps it's better not to pay any of them.

As stated previously, states differ, but in Oregon, for instance, judgments remain on your credit report for 10 years, and if the attorney for the creditor takes the time, a 10-year renewal is an option, making it 20. In Ohio it's 5 years, renewable indefinitely. What could be worse than renewable indefinitely? Of course, there are paid and unpaid judgments, with paid judgments being less severe. They are severe nonetheless. Unsatisfied charge-offs (ones that you still owe money on) are also quite severe. If your credit is picture perfect except for a combination of two judgments or unsatisfied charge-offs, you will likely have significant trouble obtaining any credit at all.

If you cannot get all of your creditors to agree to terms that are favorable, that doesn't necessarily mean that you shouldn't pay any of them. It just means that you must look at your particular circumstances and decide. If you find that "hold-outs" to your proposals are making the entire plan unworkable, think carefully before you pay any of the debts. Some scenarios are so extreme that it doesn't make sense to pay any of them. These are situations where the total debt is so high and the number of creditors so great that settling with a few doesn't help at all. In these rare circumstances, bankruptcy is certainly an option.

You may find yourself in a situation where you owe far more than you have—for example, you owe $250,000 but can only come up with $40,000 after liquidating assets. Are there many creditors? Have any of them filed suit yet? How long can you stay afloat with a lot of debt and an income stream that doesn't meet the demand or a job that has come into question altogether? Perhaps a business failure has hurt you; all of these issues may make your financial situation untenable, and a single creditor that fails to meet your repair framework may throw the whole thing into doubt.

Unless *all* of the creditors agree to favorable terms (i.e., to reduce not the monthly payment but the total amounts owed *and* remove the bad credit), then bankruptcy could be the better option. Why? Look at it this way: If you have to liquidate all of your assets to pay off creditors, only to end up with "paid collection account" reported on some or all of your accounts, then how is this better than a bankruptcy? Yes, if you do the bankruptcy wrong, then it might be better than bankruptcy, but if you do it right—by planning ahead and putting your money into assets that are immune to seizure (this differs from state to state), you could come out ahead.

Always look into the future. In 24 months, what will the situation be, based on the actions you take today? Often the choice is bad credit + no money vs. bad credit + money. Which would you rather have?

See what creditors see, and think about how they'll view

*your future report.* Another example of an unworkable credit repair plan is one that would leave you with an unpaid judgment(s) on your report, or a bad debt(s) that is unsatisfied (unpaid). Think about it. If you were a potential lender, would you rather lend to someone with a bankruptcy that is two years old or someone with one or two unsatisfied judgments that are seven years old? Lenders simply won't lend to you until you have paid your existing creditors, even if you are looking for secured money for a house or car. Those unpaid bills haunt you for seven years, and the unpaid judgments will haunt you for many more. Although a bankruptcy will haunt you for ten, you may get to keep some money/assets when you file, *and* you can obtain conventional financing to buy a house or anything else after two years (if you've reestablished good credit in accordance with this book). Choose the lesser of the evils relevant to your particular situation so that you can get on with your life. Can you buy time? Moving to a "homestead" state like Florida before declaring bankruptcy can enable you to keep your home . . . no matter what the equity or the value.

> **Note:** A good bankruptcy attorney will help you maneuver your way into keeping some or all of what you own, by simply liquidating your assets before you file and moving the cash into exempt positions. In some cases, IRAs, real estate, and other types of assets have high exemptions in certain states. Always talk to an attorney in your state before you do anything. (The state in which you file will be the state where you spent the majority of the last 180 days.)

Don't be disheartened by my references to bankruptcy; your chances for credit removal are good in nearly all cases, and very few people will ever have to take that route. In fact, many people believe that bankruptcy is their only option, yet in most cases it's not a viable option at all. Since you have several courses of action in virtually every scenario, if one thing doesn't work you will be able to try another. This puts you in a good position for getting the results you want. It's even better that you know and by now have practiced the art of negotiation. You will take all of your knowledge and skill and bring it to bear on what you seek.

## YOUR FIRST COURSE OF ACTION:
## GET THE CRA TO REMOVE THE NEGATIVE ITEM

If you think an item is there in error or is unwarranted because of extenuating circumstances, your first course of action would be to dispute the item with the CRA(s) reporting it, using one of the sample letters provided in Appendix A. (Always, always use the insurance method!) If the CRAs cannot demonstrate that the item is legitimate, then the law requires that it be removed. They have 30 days to come up with proof from the creditor or remove it from your file. Often, when they contact the creditor, the creditor will simply be too busy to respond! Yes, even the worst of credit can be removed this way. This is often the best course, since it only costs you the price of a stamp! Send a request letter, wait 30 days, and if that fails, send a demand letter.

Your chances will depend on what type of item it is (car loan, credit card, etc.) and whether or not the item is paid. Creditors are more likely to ignore requests from CRAs if the item is paid since it costs them time and money to respond. But they often get busy and things will fall through the cracks! Remember, as stated in the things you must know section, don't dispute more than two or three items at once, since it will raise red flags. One at a time is best.

## YOUR SECOND COURSE OF ACTION:
## NEGOTIATE DIRECTLY WITH THE CREDITOR

If the CRA fails to respond in your favor, you can go directly to the creditor in an attempt to have the item removed through negotiating. At many stages of lateness, the creditor will often have turned the debt over to a collection agency. This happens if a debt goes past 90 days. Now, if a collection agency has it, they will try to collect whatever they can, since they get a commission on what is paid. If they don't collect anything from you, they don't get paid. At this stage of the game, the collection agency is only expecting to collect 15 to 20 percent of whatever is owed. That is the national average. Keep this in mind when negotiating with them.

There is nothing at all wrong with dealing with a collection agency, providing it behaves properly and you are making progress. If not, then you can take a course of action to have the matter referred back to the creditor, as outlined in Chapter 4: Dealing with Collectors.

As you already know, some marks on your report are worse than others. In addition to that aspect of things, certain situations will give you higher leverage than others. For example, if you have a rating of R9, which is considered a bad debt (the worst), you may think that would be the hardest to remove. Sometimes it is, but sometimes not. Why? Because if it's this bad you probably still owe money, which gives you leverage in negotiating a deal. You see, you have their money, which they want, and when someone wants something, that gives you some power. You can negotiate this off, and I have personally done so, not once but twice! Your goal is negotiating a deal with the creditor (or collection agency) that will accomplish one of the following, listed in order of desirability:

- The account is changed from a negative to a positive rating.
- The account is removed from your credit report entirely.
- The current rating is replaced with one based on future performance.
- The account is changed from negative to neutral.

When negotiating, always ask for the best deal first, so you can have a place in the middle to meet should you get resistance. That is, ask that the rating be changed to positive from negative since they might say yes right away. If they say no, keep trying for that high point, going up the chain of command if you feel you need to. (Don't ask to go higher if the negotiations are going well, as this can squelch your chances at getting a good deal and delay any settlement at all. Don't get too greedy!) In any case, by aiming high in the beginning you still have a middle place you can meet, which is still very desirable. Your goal is to elevate your score, so what you really want is to remove the bad credit.

### Situations Where Money Is Owed

You already know that this is the best scenario, since you have leverage. Contact the creditor and simply tell them that you want to pay them, but you need them to remove the bad credit so you can get on with your life. Appeal to their emotions, but also tell them that you are willing to make good. If you want, depending on the stage that it is in, you can negotiate a settlement lower than the full amount in addition to the removal of the bad credit. What kind of settlement? Usually it can range anywhere from 30 to 70 cents on the dollar. Again, this will depend on the stage that it's in and to whom it is owed. At the collection agency stage on closed accounts you will get good results, since the agency isn't expecting but 15 to 20 cents on the dollar anyway. People just want money; they don't care what your report looks like if they can get their money. Would they like to see your report hinder you ad infinitum? Sure, some people are that vindictive, but not always at the expense of their money!

> *Tip:* Always remember, once you pay them you have used your chips. Don't pay until you have what you want. You must get them to state, in writing and succinctly, that they will "remove all derogatory information regarding the account from your credit report" once the account is paid in full. If they agree to the terms and send you the letter, make sure that you read it carefully. Often they'll say one thing on the phone and then send you something that doesn't resemble what they agreed to. Their letter will

*often say things like "Paid Account" or something simi-lar. This is not the same as removing the item from the report because it is still derogatory information that will lower your credit score. Furthermore, regardless of what the letter states, they'll sometimes refuse to remove the information in accordance with the agreement, in which case you'll have to sue. You can always provide proof of payment to the CRAs yourself, but they'll likely report the item as prescribed by the creditor anyway, unless you sue them as well. Read Chapter 7: Courts: A Useful and Viable Option.*

I'm going to give you a couple of real-life examples of how negative information was removed while money was still owed.

### EXAMPLE A

A major credit card was issued from a large national bank. It was a credit card I got back in college when I didn't understand the value of good credit. Sound familiar? It was an R6, which is pretty bad. I contacted the card issuer, managed to talk to the right person, and made a deal: I'll pay them what I owe ($600) if they remove the negative credit rating. They agreed, and it was that simple. I got the deal in writing of course, using the insurance method that I spoke of in Chapter 1: The Rules of the Game.

### EXAMPLE B

I had another major credit card on which I still owed $900, reported as R9. I negotiated a deal wherein I would pay the balance and they would in turn report it as unrated. This is a little-known tactic in negotiating credit repair, since most peo-ple don't know about it, including the creditor!

**Note:** In all negotiations, you never make what you really want the starting point. Although what I did here was a victory since it's not negative, it's much better to have it rated as never late or taken off entirely. Why? Because positive is good for credit scoring. Also, if it's not rated but is still on the report, a potential lender might call to try and find out the exact history, which can end up bad. Hence, you start with asking for a lot when you negotiate, and your last resort is accepting the unrated. It happened!

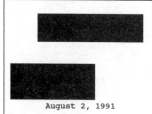

August 2, 1991

Dana Neal
3045 Morestown Court North
Columbus, OH 43224

RE: ████████████████
     ████236 336

Dear Mr. Neal:

In the interest of good customer service, the Bank has notified its applicable credit bureaus to reflect your account as follows:

"Account Closed/Zero Balance/Not Rated By Credit Grantor".

Kindly allow four to six weeks for the bureaus to comply with our request.

Very truly yours,

Supervisor
External Recoveries

REH:ss

## Cases Where Money Is Not Owed

This is tougher, but it can still be done. Some real-life examples:

## EXAMPLE C

A credit card issuer reported an R7. I didn't owe them any money and had no leverage. It took me a year to find and negotiate a deal with the right person (the VP of credit management, in this case). The deal? I open a secured card with a $300 limit, never miss a payment on the card for 12 months, and they remove any negative history on the old card, giving it an unrated. (Don't believe it? See the illustration below.)

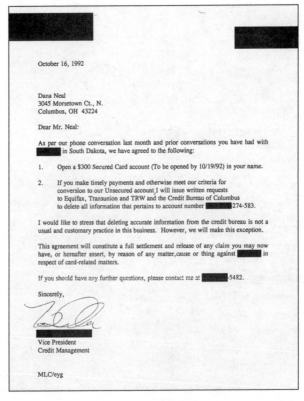

October 16, 1992

Dana Neal
3045 Morsetown Ct., N.
Columbus, OH 43224

Dear Mr. Neal:

As per our phone conversation last month and prior conversations you have had with ██████ in South Dakota, we have agreed to the following:

1.  Open a $300 Secured Card account (To be opened by 10/19/92) in your name.

2.  If you make timely payments and otherwise meet our criteria for conversion to our Unsecured account I will issue written requests to Equifax, Transunion and TRW and the Credit Bureau of Columbus to delete all information that pertains to account number ████ 274-583.

I would like to stress that deleting accurate information from the credit bureau is not a usual and customary practice in this business. However, we will make this exception.

This agreement will constitute a full settlement and release of any claim you may now have, or hereafter assert, by reason of any matter, cause or thing against ██████ in respect of card-related matters.

If you should have any further questions, please contact me at ████ -5482.

Sincerely,

Vice President
Credit Management

MLC/eyg

Convince the creditor that it's in their best interest, since they get a new long-term customer that has learned his or her lesson, and it doesn't hurt anyone. It's good customer service. You're going to be around for a while, and the bank can benefit from having you as a customer. It also gives you a happy meeting ground, since they don't have to report good things about you when they really don't want to. Was a year of negotiating worth it? You better believe it! That would have stayed on for another four years, seven total years, and would have prevented me from doing all sorts of things during that time.

> **Note:** This major bank also tried to get out of its promise after the year expired. Had I not had the deal in writing and forced the issue, I would have been out of luck. The person who made the deal was very cold and avoided my calls, but I kept calling every three or four days, leaving messages explaining that I wasn't going to go away and I expected him to live up to his agreement. Just when I had fished a letter threatening legal action (after about 30 days of the runaround), he finally answered my call and agreed to provide a letter requesting removal to the CRAs. That's why you use the insurance method!

### EXAMPLE D

Another large credit card issuer listed an R6 rating, and I again didn't owe any money and therefore lacked leverage. Would you believe that I got no for an answer about 10 times before I talked with someone who said yes? In fact, I even got more than I asked for! You see, I asked to open a secured card for six months in return for their removing the old negative information as long as I paid on time. The guy said, "That won't be necessary, we'll open you up a new account right now and remove any reference to the old account right away." No kidding. Can you believe it? It really happened: See the illustration below. Surreal.

April 29, 1992

DANA NEAL

3045 MORSETOWN CT NORTH
COLUMBUS            OH    43224

Account: █████████1001
Social Security: █████████

Dear DANA NEAL:

This letter will confirm your recent inquiry regarding your above █████████████Card account.

Please be advised that we have deleted all information released to the credit reporting agencies regarding this account.

We sincerely regret any inconvenience you may have experienced.

Sincerely,

Credit Bureau Unit
Accounts Control Department

bf

Any variations of payment terms can be sought, and you can even get new extended payment terms on open accounts or accounts not yet in collections.

### EXAMPLE E

There are many lessons to be learned from a single encounter. I advise you to read this example carefully and glean the many lessons contained within it. The following is an actual conversation (summarized) I had with a creditor (not a collection agency), and it is the rule, not the exception. I will change the names to protect the guilty:

**Me:** Hello, how are you today?

**Mr. Smith:** I'm fine. What can I do for you?

**Me:** Yes, sir. Well, I'm calling to talk with you about my account, and wish to come up with a way in which I can settle it amicably.

**Mr. Smith:** Sounds good. I see here that you previously offered a 25-percent settlement on your debt. We are prepared to take 50 percent, but no less. Your account will charge-off unless you pay the bill by the end of next month.

**Note:** A charge-off usually occurs after six months without paying. It is where the creditor no longer expects to receive money for the debt and charges off the debt on the books. The creditor, in turn, receives a tax deduction from the government for the loss (I don't know what this amount is, but it must be below 25 percent because before a charge-off, creditors will take a 25-percent settlement. If they thought the charge-off would be more profitable than taking $2,500 on a $10,000 debt, then they would never take 25 percent and lose out on the tax benefit of a charge-off. Keep in mind that this does not apply to tax-exempt credit unions). They no longer expect to ever receive any money for the debt, so whatever they receive is welcome. In addition, have no fear of this common tactic of a collector saying "a charge-off is imminent." Your position is not really hampered by a charge-off. What's the sense in agreeing to something you don't want anyway?

> **Me:** I understand. I have other creditors who are also demanding money, and I can only afford to pay some of them. Therefore, I must pay those who give me the best settlement deal. There are others willing to settle for 25 percent, and I'm sorry for this situation, but if it comes down to paying 50 percent or 25 percent, I'm going to have to choose the 25-percent deal.
>
> **Mr. Smith:** Then we will send it to our legal department, and they will take action against you.
>
> **Me:** With all due respect, Mr. Smith, I'd like to take this matter up the chain of command. I understand that you are just doing your job, but I'd like to take the matter up with your supervisor. What is his name?
>
> **Mr. Smith:** His name is Mr. Brindle, but he will not tell you anything different than what I just told you.
>
> **Me:** I understand. Just the same, I'd like to speak with him if you don't mind. I understand that you are trying to do your job and it's nothing personal.
>
> **Mr. Smith:** What for? He is going to tell you the exact same thing that I just told you. You are wasting our time here. We will not take less than 50 percent under any circumstances.

**Note:** See what happened here? This person won't budge, and besides, he's a front-line crony anyway, without the power to give me what I asked for. Further, he's an ass in spite of my cordial demeanor.

> **Me:** Look, I've asked nicely to speak with your supervisor, and there is nothing wrong with that request.

He hung up on me.

**Note:** Get the picture? These people are jerks. However, you have to buckle down and be persistent, because you aren't going to get what you want unless you make it happen. Nobody will settle your problems for you, and nobody cares. It's all up to you. Perseverance.

> I called back with a plan to ask for the head of the department. In this case, the department I was dealing with is actually separate from the collection department. How do I know this? I had already spent several hours talking with various people in the collection department, asking them who could approve settlements. Can you imagine what it took to get the number for that department? It takes work, and you just keep calling and asking until you get the answer you want. Remember, you have to talk directly with a decision maker, nobody else will do. Nobody!

A woman answered.

> **Me:** With whom am I speaking please?
> **Jennifer:** Jennifer.
> **Me:** Can I get your last name please?
> **Jennifer:** I'm sorry, I don't give that out.
> (Typical)

**Me:** I understand; how about a last initial or your operator number?

**Jennifer:** L.

**Me:** Thank you. Now Miss, could you please tell me who is the head of your division?

**Jennifer:** Well, we have several supervisors here.

**Me:** I would like to know who the head of the department is.

**Jennifer:** I don't quite know how to answer that.

**Me:** Let me put it this way: What is the position, or title, of Mr. Brindle?

**Jennifer:** He is a supervisor.

**Me:** OK. Who is his supervisor?

**Jennifer:** Supervisors work for team leaders. His team leader is Paula.

**Me:** Paula who?

**Jennifer:** If she wants to tell you that she can herself.

**Me:** All right. Is she available to speak with please?

**Jennifer:** What is your name and account number?

(I give it to her.)

**Jennifer:** Hold on.

(I was placed on hold for about three minutes.)

**Gruff Voice:** Hello, this is Mr. Brindle. How can I help you?

**Me:** Yes, hello. My name is Neal, and I've asked to speak with team leader Paula.

**Mr. Brindle:** Well, I know who you are, and you are talking to me. How can I help you?

**Me:** With all due respect, I did not ask for you. Please transfer me to Paula.

**Mr. Brindle:** That isn't going to happen. If you want a settlement, you are going to have to deal with me.

**Me:** I asked to speak to Paula, and you refuse to transfer me?

**Mr. Brindle:** That's right. I'm making the decisions around here.

**Me:** I've asked to speak to your supervisor, and that is a reasonable request.

**Mr. Brindle:** I don't care. Now what do you want to do about your account?

**Me:** I tell you what. I will agree to speak with you about my account, but I reserve the right to speak with Paula if we cannot come to an amicable arrangement.

**Mr. Brindle:** No! It's not going to happen.

**Me:** Look, I telephoned your bank in order to make settlement arrangements, and I get treated like this? We are finished.

I hang up. I call back and ask the person who answers to speak with Paula. I explained that I don't wish to be transferred to anyone else unless they are senior to Paula or a team leader. I am adamant about my request. A few minutes pass, and a woman answers.

**Woman:** Hello Mr. Neal, my name is Miss Casic. How can I help you?

**Me:** Well, I don't know if you can or not. I asked to speak with Paula or someone with her authority. Would you be that person?

**Miss Casic:** I can approve any decision that comes through this office.

**Me:** Good. Let me first start by saying that I'm unhappy with my treatment by your colleagues. (I ran the gamut of my conversations with Brindle and Smith.) It's not unreasonable for me to ask for a superior if I don't get the answer I am looking for. This treatment is uncalled for, and it is I who called your department in an attempt to settle this matter. If someone asks to speak with a supervisor, the policy should be clear that they should be placed on hold and the superior found immediately.

**Miss Casic:** I agree.

**Me:** Very good. Now, here is my situation . . .

I briefly explained my circumstances . . . taking responsibility for the problem, stating why I became late (you use whatever good reason, or combination of reasons, you can come up with here, e.g., losing a job, becoming disabled, etc.), and explaining that I have other debts and could not pay them all (but would pay the ones on which I was able to get the best settlement), and so on.

*Tip: Remember, there is a stark difference between reasons and excuses, between whining and explaining. Stay real, and stay professional.*

I informed her that I'd been offered a 50-percent settlement by her bank but it just wasn't possible, especially considering that I've been offered 25-percent settlements from others. When she asked who they were, I explained that I could not tell her due to confidentiality agreements I had with the creditors. She pressed and tried (using my credit report, which was in front of her) to get me to tell her, but I argued that for the purposes of the settlement with her bank, what occurred with other creditors was not relevant and would not help the bank's bottom line.

She told me she would review the case and asked if she could have my telephone number. I explained that because I was inundated with collectors, I'd had to change my number. I ask her to not take offense but said that I could not give it out. I told her I'd be glad to call her back at the time of her choosing. We agreed that I would call her back in two hours. When I called her back, she offered a 40-percent settlement. I explained that I appreciated her working with me and I knew she was trying. However, I said I could not justify settling with her bank for 40 percent when I could settle with others for 25 percent. She tried again to find out with whom I'd settled on those terms, and I used the same excuse as to why I could not.

I apologized for not being able to settle with her bank, especially considering the special attention she had given my case. I said that if I could pay all of my creditors the balance owed, I would gladly do it, but that I just was not in a position to do it because the total amount owed was far more than I had. Furthermore, I explained, the money I was using to settle with was borrowed money, and I would have to pay that back as well.

When I attempted to close the conversation and get off the phone, she said that she would like to look at my situation more closely and asked if I would call her back tomorrow.

When I called her back, she agreed to accept 25 percent. This amounted to roughly $6,000. (Yes, the original balance was $24,000!) The deal stipulated that I would be required to pay the balance within 30 days. Great? Well, almost. Remember, there's still that little matter of the poor credit. If I settled with the bank, it would automatically show up on my credit report as a "Paid Settlement," a derogatory item (better than a charge-off, but derogatory).

I thanked Miss Casic for working with me and told her how much this would help me to get out from under this debt. Then, very naively, I asked what would happen to my credit report. She told me it would show "Paid Settlement." I asked, "That's bad, isn't it?" She said it wasn't good but was better than a charge-off. I sighed and then asked if there was something that could be done about that, to which she said no.

*Tip:* *Never, ever mention that you are using a credit repair technique. If you do, you will surely fail no mat-*

*ter what you say after that. Put on your poker face: you are a novice at credit but are a fast learner and are very concerned about it.*

"Hmmm," I said. "It seems to me that we have a settlement here, one that is acceptable to both of us." I continued, "Would you consider removing the derogatory information in this account?" "No. We can't change it." I replied, "I see. Well, this concerns me. It doesn't seem to benefit the bank in any way to keep the derogatory history on there, and it seems punitive. I don't want to seem ungrateful for all of your efforts, but I have to take all things into account when I settle with my various creditors."

> **Tip:** *Remember the situational approach from "The Art of Negotiation"? The only thing that you can tell from the dialogue is that she was both logical and reasonable. The tone of her voice said the same, yet while she was mostly all business, she was interested in my story. Like most people, she wasn't going to respond to whining; I used equal doses of logic and tempered emotion in order to win her over.*

She then said, "Banks use information to assess credit risk, and my bank cannot list your account as positive, since that would be seen as endorsing you as a risk."

I explained that it would be good business for both of us if we could settle this account, deleting the derogatory credit as well. After listening carefully, she said, "I hear what you are saying. However, I have responsibilities to this bank and when it comes time for auditing, how can I justify this action? The many settlement accounts that come through this office are all approved by me and are looked at by people higher than me, even though I make decisions."

I explained that I would need time to consider my options and talk to an attorney, then get back to her. I then sent her an e-mail later that day:

I understand your comments about endorsing a credit risk. I do see your point, but there is something else that must be considered when assessing risk. That is, what is true today may not be true tomorrow. Yes, I failed to pay the debt as agreed, but there were extenuating, life-altering circumstances that led to my financial situation. This was an occurrence outside of my control. The risk and credit extended were based on a large income that came to an abrupt end. Yes, my creditworthiness has changed, but only as a function of how much credit to extend, not whether or not I am a good risk.

Someone looking at my creditworthiness today, in effect, does not see the same person that your bank initially saw when it extended me credit. This should be taken into account when creditors assess my current and future risk, but creditors don't see that; they only see my current credit report. The current state of credit reporting only reports whether or not something was paid and when. The implication of the whole system is based on one yardstick: people pay or don't pay based on their character (and all that that entails). You and I both know that this measure is far too simplistic.

On the subject of your internal audits, I understand that you have those. But auditors don't look at every single file, they only look at a few random files, and this is probably only performed quarterly. The chances of this becoming an issue are very small. Furthermore, even if it was discovered, you could justify the action based on my history and on the basis that you are doing what is in the best interest of the bank. It certainly wouldn't be the first time. Besides, you are paid to make those decisions.

> **Tip:** *Give a couple of days in between conversations. You don't want to seem pushy or too exited, and you want them to think about you as a person and your situation. By the same token, don't wait more than three days, as bank supervisors are busy people and will begin to forget about you.*

This was the heart of my e-mail, and I closed it by pleading with her to understand. When I called her three days later, I explained that my lawyer said that removing the negative information was okay, and that this is often done in settlement agreements. (People with debts often have lawyers, so it should have come as no surprise that I was talking to one.) She refused to budge. I told her that I'd gotten another creditor to agree to it remove it, and added, "I understand that it's my fault that this has occurred; however, whom does it benefit to leave the bad mark on the report? It doesn't benefit the bank, and it only hurts me." She said that the bank would not remove it, to which I responded, "I appreciate your willingness to take 25 percent on this account, and your time in trying to settle the matter. The issue of the credit report disturbs me, and I have to consider all factors when settling with the various creditors. I want to settle with your bank, but there are others willing to go a little farther by removing the derogatory mark. I still fail to see why I'm being penalized when we are settling. (Notice the positive, unambiguous remark: we are settling.) I ask you to please reconsider, since the bad mark does not benefit the bank in any way, and removing it costs the bank nothing." She still wouldn't budge, and then I offered her a compromise.

I said, "I have a compromise that my attorney told me about—one that may satisfy both of our needs. I'll agree to pay the 25-percent settlement and, in exchange, the bank will report the account as nonrated (unrated), or R0. This, while not giving me a positive rating and increasing my credit score, does not reflect badly. It neither helps nor hinders my credit score, since it is neutral. The bank can get its money, and I don't get penalized for seven years for the mistake." She said that she was unaware of such a rating (which is common), but she would check with her credit-reporting department. She asked if I would call her back on Monday so she could have time to research it, and I agreed (it was a Thursday).

I called her back, and she said that she could not change the reporting unless I paid the entire balance, which is quite common. What did I do? That's not important, what's important is what would *you* do? It depends on your situation—how many accounts you have in arrears, what your credit report looks like otherwise, how much money you have, and.

You could settle with her for 25 percent + bad credit or 100 percent + no bad credit. You could thank her for her time and for her hard work and walk away, wait for the bank's attorney to contact you, and then try for a better settlement with the attorney. Does this bank sell its debts to collection agencies? If so, maybe you would be better off to take one of these two options right now. How is your sanity? If you've come this far, can you handle starting over with a third party who purchased the debt or a crony that works for a two-bit collection attorney? Only you can decide.

> **Note:** Usually, creditors want 80 percent or more in order to perform the bad credit removal. More often, a 25-percent deal plus bad credit removal is only going to occur after legal proceedings are about to commence and the discussions are with a lawyer.

### A Word about Autos

Automobiles can of course be repossessed. Many consumers are duped into thinking that if they give the car back voluntarily then it's paid off. Not so. The car will be sold at auction and the amount applied to your loan, then you will owe the difference plus late fees and interest. This will still show as repossession on your credit report as well. If this hasn't yet happened, contact the creditor and state that you have financial problems but do intend to pay. Ask for an extension.

Often you can get the terms of your loan renegotiated at a lower payment for a longer term and at a higher interest payment. If the car has been taken already and you owe a balance, simply attempt to negotiate a deal to settle for 25 percent of the balance and removal of negative credit. Be steadfast, and they will likely get tired of you and settle. Negotiate the best deal possible, and, as always, don't walk away when you've been offered a good deal or when legal action against you would likely commence if you failed to take the deal.

Was the auto unreliable? If so, and the seller also provided the financing, see Chapter 7: Court—A Useful and Viable Option.

## Getting Judgments Removed

A judgment is really just a piece of paper—a court document that says someone owes someone money. Having a judgment on your report can be a real showstopper, even with a substantial amount of good credit. If you think a judgment is unwarranted because of extenuating circumstances, your first course of action is to dispute the item with the CRA, using one of the sample letters provided in Appendix A.

If the CRA cannot demonstrate that it is in fact legitimate, then the law requires that it be removed. You may or may not be aware of the circumstances surrounding the judgment, as it could have been awarded in absentia (e.g., you were not present at the hearing or failed to respond to a lawsuit, so you lost by default). In any case, when you begin disputing it with the CRA, ask them to provide specific documentation to back up the legitimacy of the judgment, information you may find helpful when you are attempting to have it removed. Which court is it in? What's the case number? Perhaps you don't have a copy of the judgment. If not, get one from the court as soon as you can.

> **Note:** As stated in the section about public records, service bureaus are notorious for making mistakes, including transcribing Social Security numbers incorrectly. If you think that a judgment is on your report in error, simply send a letter to the CRA(s) demanding that they remove it. If they fail to comply, you'll likely find some useful information in Chapter 7: Court—A Useful and Viable Option.

### Unpaid Judgments

Surely a judgment on which you still owe money will look worse on your credit file than one that has been paid. The former is called an unsatisfied (unpaid) judgment, but it's not a cause for alarm. Actually, owing money gives you leverage in negotiating a settlement. If the CRA continues to report the judgment and can substantiate it, then your next course of action is to contact the person/company that sued you (plaintiff) and negotiate a deal for a partial or full settlement. Most people will take a partial payment since they would rather have something than nothing. Remember to be nice. (As a last resort, explain that you wish to settle because the judgment is hurting you, and reason with them: it will do the plaintiff no good to have the derogatory information remain on your credit report once you both settle. This is a last resort because you don't want to give the plaintiff any ammunition in your negotiations.) Offer 20 percent of the judgment and work your way up in small bits from there. Maybe you can get off with paying 25 to 50 percent! In return, the plaintiff agrees to a stipulation to your payment, wherein he or she "sets aside the judgment" in exchange for your cash.

Explain to the plaintiff that this will require his filing papers (stipulating that the judgment is set aside), but that you know how to do it and will handle that part of it. Since each state's respective laws are different, I cannot provide you with a sample stipulation. A judge will not approve it anyway unless it is correct (i.e., adheres to your state laws). It's a good idea to go to your local courthouse and talk to the civil clerk. The clerk will probably send you to the file room, but ask for a sample of a Stipulation to Set Aside Judgment, and that way you will have a template to work from so you will get the format and the language right!

Be sure the stipulation includes all of the information necessary for a judge to sign it. For instance, you must include your name and address, identify yourself as the defendant, provide a signature block for yourself, and include all of the same for the plaintiff. In addition, you'll need to include the original judgment's case number, court, and so on. Title this document "Stipulation to Set

Aside Judgment" and place exactly what the settlement agreement is in the body copy. Send it to the plaintiff and let him or her know that it must be notarized at the time of signing. Provide a self-addressed stamped envelope to make it easy to return it to you.

Make a certified true copy of the document that is signed by the plaintiff, using a notary. This is just in case the court loses it and the plaintiff has a change of heart or dies! You then file the stipulation with the court, again supplying a self-addressed stamped envelope and requesting that it be used to provide you with a copy of the stipulation once the judge signs it. The settlement is not complete until the judge signs the stipulation!

Once you receive the stipulation with the judge's signature, make a copy for the CRAs and send it to them right away, demanding that the judgment be removed. Keep the original for yourself, placing it in your permanent files.

If you're confused or unsure and need help, contact an attorney and explain what you're trying to do. Attorneys can assist you in this process, usually for a nominal fee. If an attorney doesn't know what a Stipulation to Set Aside Judgment is, then find one that does.

### Paid Judgments

If the judgment is paid, make sure that it is reported as such. Having an unpaid judgment on your credit report will certainly hurt your credit score, so provide proof to the CRAs that it was paid if you have it. Whether you have proof or not, you still want to get the plaintiff to provide a Stipulation to Set Aside Judgment (following the procedures outlined above). The plaintiff should be cooperative, since you already paid him or her. Be nice! It's *your* problem, and you have no leverage to make the other party sign anything.

If you meet a lot of resistance in getting a stipulation, then settle for getting the plaintiff to report the judgment correctly if it's paid but reported unpaid. Explain that you simply want the facts presented on your credit report, and he or she is responsible for that happening.

Of course, if you do have proof that the judgment was paid, then simply provide it to the CRAs and demand that the judgment be reported as satisfied.

### What if You Can't Get It Removed?

Don't worry; if you're unable to get a judgment removed, it's not the end of the world! Keep trying with all of your creditors and remember to put as much distance between you and the bad credit as you can, by paying your bills on time and reestablishing credit. You should consider exercising your right to place a statement of up to 100 words that explains the situation in your credit file.

### Removing Inquiries

Inquiries are bad news. Because they are factored into your credit score, they can and will affect your ability to get credit, regardless of how good your credit is. Basically, anything over two inquiries per year will often get you denied. Since they stay on your report for two years, inquiries can be a thorn in the side of consumers who have otherwise flawless reports.

There are two types of inquiries on every report. One type is there for everyone to see (public), and this is a case where you've applied for credit. Another type (private) is not supposed to show up on your credit report and will only be seen by you. (The terms *public* and *private* are terms used by me, not the CRAs.)

The latter type can include the following:

- A promotional inquiry in response to which only your name and address are provided. Basically, the CRAs sell your name and address to third parties, and you end up on a mailing list since you meet certain lending criteria. If you wish to opt out of this (not be solicited), simply send a letter to the three CRAs demanding that you not receive

these solicitations. Use the insurance method, in all things. (These inquiries remain for 12 months.)
* Periodic reviews occur when current creditors pull your credit file. (These inquiries remain for 12 months.)
* A request you have made to review your credit file.
* Requests you have made to update or change your report and to receive a copy of the updated report.

When accounts enter collections, creditors will often continue to make periodic review inquiries in order to obtain information about you. They want to know as much as they can, and your credit report will often provide useful information, such as how much money you make, where you live, and what your other debts are. Unfortunately, this is legal. Banks have made it part of their standard contracts, and it's the consumers that are harmed by repeated inquiries. In my view, it's hideous; I'm hoping that one day the practice becomes illegal.

One of the big problems with periodic reviews is that CRAs very often fail to properly categorize such inquiries, so they often end up on your public inquiry list. Fortunately, there are some things you can do to get them removed from your report. There are three courses of action you can take. Simply try one, and if that doesn't work, try the others.

1) Send a demand letter to the CRA explaining that you did not authorize the inquiry and you want it to be removed. If you know that the CRA made a mistake, since the inquiry came from an existing creditor and was a periodic review, be sure and spell that out in your letter. As stated in the beginning of this chapter, CRAs are required to contact the creditor to verify the legitimacy of an item per your request. This includes inquiries. Since creditors are notoriously busy with other fish to fry, it is unlikely that they will respond to the CRA. Remember, creditors have 30 days to respond, and if they fail to do so the CRA must remove the derogatory item in accordance with the FCRA. Wait 30 days. If the first letter fails, then send a second

demand letter to the CRA. Sometimes the CRA will simply delete the item if you threaten legal action. The CRAs are interested in making money, not battling with you.

2) If the first step above doesn't work, send a letter to the creditor demanding that it be removed. Explain that the periodic review inquiry is not supposed to show up on your credit report, since you never requested an extension or an increase of credit. Wait 30 days. If that doesn't work, send a second demand letter.

3) If that fails, find a good lawyer (have him agree to a flat fee up front; it shouldn't be more than a one-hour charge of $150 to $250) to write the demand letter to the CRA and the creditor. If it doesn't work, have him send a second demand letter. That will usually work, since CRAs and creditors will take a letter from a lawyer more seriously than from you, and they don't want legal action since it doesn't pay them anything.

Refer to Appendix A for sample letters regarding inquiries. If all else fails and you know for a fact (and can prove) that the inquiry is a periodic review and should not be part of your public inquiry list, consider filing suit.

> **Tip:** Always be cognizant that applying for any type of credit generates an inquiry, even overdraft protection! So never apply for credit unless absolutely necessary, and only when you're assured of approval.

### When You Get the Deal

Get the deal in writing before providing the creditor with the settlement funds. Mark the check or money order with "paid in full" in the memo block, and be sure to follow up in 90 days by obtaining a copy of your report and verifying that the change in reporting has occurred.

> **Note:** If you have agreed to settle with the original creditor while the matter is still in the hands of the

agency, make sure that you word the settlement in such a manner as to include not only "all credit reporting agencies to be notified to remove negative marks" but also "the relevant collection agency to be notified to delete the marks from its database and stop reporting it to the credit reporting agencies." As with all agreements, if you get the deal and then they go back on it, hound them for 30 days, then sue for damages (see Chapter 7). Remember, you've been harmed, and the best way to deal with it is to force them into fessing up to their sins.

## FOR THOSE WHO CAN'T BUY THEIR WAY OUT

A couple of options: 1) Negotiate a deal where you pay it off in stages. 2) Work hard and save your money, and then use it to pay your creditors off. You owe it, right? 3) Borrow the money from someone else to pay the creditor, either a lending institution or friend/family member.

You could go see the president of your local bank, explain the situation, tell him you have a job, that you've changed or the situation has changed, and that you want to get an installment loan to pay off these creditors. He or she can even send the money directly to the creditors you owe. Take a copy of your credit report with you; show that you're not afraid, that you're just trying to fulfill your obligations. Heck, try three or four banks. I once went to four banks before I got a car loan with bad credit! Sometimes small banks or credit unions work best. Agree to open a savings and checking account with their bank. Whatever it takes.

### The Key

You see, it's all about negotiating. You start out giving a little here and there, and see what happens. You overcome objections by giving a little, appealing to their good nature, explaining your mistake, giving a little more, agreeing that you did wrong, giving a little more . . .

From 1991 to 1992, only once in my nine attempts at getting negative information removed did I fail, and that was with a very small bank in a small town. (The president of the bank was a very mean, vindictive old man, and I wasn't going to change his mind.) Remember what I said earlier about reasonable people?

I learned something from every single interaction and used it in the next. Every person you contact will be different. Some will be nice, others not. But in all cases, be nice, because that's what works. If you can't get the answer you want, take it to the person's supervisor. Be respectful and ask to speak with someone higher up the chain. Someone will say yes in most cases! Just be persistent, and don't give up!

Come up with an action plan for what you're going to say before you ever make the first call. Take notes before you ever pick up the phone, and carefully record whom you spoke with, what was said, and when. Get their direct extension and address as well. Be methodical. You see, there's no secret; it's just knowing all the rules of the game, and then negotiating. That's it!

## WHAT IF YOU CAN'T MAKE A DEAL?

You will not likely fail if you follow the guidelines in the book. People rarely fail when using these techniques; in fact, everyone I have spoken with who has used the methods outlined in this book has succeeded. But if for some reason you fail, don't worry; it's not the end of the world! Keep trying with all of your creditors, and remember to put as much distance between you and the bad credit as you can, by paying your bills on time and reestablishing credit.

Here again, you should also consider exercising your right to place a statement (100 words max by law) in your credit file that explains the situation. (Make sure it's concise with substantive reasons, not whiny.) Keep in mind that this won't affect your score, but it can sometimes help if human eyes are looking at it, since it shows that you care enough about your report to make a statement.

# ▲

# CHAPTER 7

# COURT—
# A USEFUL AND
# VIABLE OPTION

When I was young, my mother always told me it was wrong to sue people. She believed that it wasn't Christian, and she was steadfast in this view, regardless of the circumstances.

If you hold this view, I certainly respect that. After all, I don't have to eat your breakfast for you. But for those who believe that there are no absolutes and that justice can be served through the courts, a lawsuit can be a useful path. If you find yourself in a situation where all other avenues have been exhausted (examples relating to credit issues might include a breach of contract, erroneous billing or credit reporting, a landlord problem, or harassment by a collection agency), then the courts can help. They are there for a reason, let's face it, and some things just don't happen unless they're made to happen; courts can make things happen.

Of course, I'm not an attorney, but I've filed my fair share of lawsuits, both as a *pro se* (representing myself) plaintiff and with representation. *Represent Yourself in Court: How to Prepare & Try a Winning Case*, by attorneys Paul Bergman and Sara J. Berman-Barrett, and Ralph E. Warner, is an excellent primer on going it alone. Armed with this book and a copy of your local court rules (the clerk of court will provide you with this), you can be quite a terror. Be sure to go to the file room of the civil court as well, since those records are open to the public and you can see exactly how things are done.

Your local legal library is also a great source of information, and it will probably have access to online services like LexisNexis and WestLaw. Useful in bringing up old case law, these can provide you with a framework for your arguments and background on how cases like yours have played out in the past.

Of course, you can always get an attorney to represent you. Just follow the guidelines for selecting and retaining a lawyer that were spelled out earlier.

## DECLARATORY JUDGMENTS

When you aren't asking for anything other than to walk away without anybody owing anything (i.e., you are not seeking damages), you can file for what is known as a "declaratory judgment." It's faster and easier to get than a "judgment." Heck, you could simply win by default if the other party (defendant) doesn't respond to the complaint. The defendant usually only has 30 days from the time he or she is served.

Further, in some states you can request this action in municipal court, which is usually less expensive than a standard civil suit (the cost averages $85), and you could get a hearing much sooner than in state circuit court (known in some states as the court of common pleas). I've been told that the wait in Ohio, as of this writing, is about six months in municipal court versus two years in the court of common pleas. It also appears that few attorneys actually know that you can use municipal court for such matters. (This may explain why the wait time is 75 percent less.) In Ohio, cases in municipal court are for suits brought that involve $15,000 or less.

Keep in mind that a declaratory judgment only works for contracts, not torts. (A contract constitutes an agreement between two or more parties to do or not do something and a right to performance of the other's duty or a remedy for the breach of the other's duty. Every other type of civil action for which damages can be brought is a tort.) In addition, although a judge may issue a "summary judgment" (where he rules without a hearing) in your favor, he will require a trial if he feels that there are items in the case that must be litigated. This isn't something to be afraid of, just aware of. If you're dead right, can prove it, and you have case law on your side, then you can go to court and stand tall all by your lonesome. Just make sure you have the local court rules and know them well—so as not to upset the judge.

> **Tip:** As stated in the section that follows, filing suit first is an excellent way to keep a lawsuit from showing up on your credit report. If you file first, even if the defendant countersues, by rule the suit cannot be placed on your report. Powerful stuff!

This type of action can also be used in other ways in some states—such as to get derogatory information removed from your credit report. For example, if a creditor reports erroneous information to a CRA and refuses to remove it, then you've probably got both a contract breach and a tort. It's likely that the terms and conditions of your creditor's contract (which you agree to when you use a credit card, for example) state that the creditor will report your account information to the CRAs. If they've done so erroneously, then it stands to reason that you have a contract breach. You probably also have a tort, since the negative information on the credit report damaged you outside the contract.

If you can make this work, not only would the offending mark on your credit report be removed, but if there is something else offending relating to the same account, it may also be removed.

For example, let's say that the creditor erroneously reports, "account closed by credit grantor," and there's something else factual on it, like "60 days late." If you can get the creditor on a breach of contract, then it's possible that the whole account as reported could be tossed. This is one of the few things I discuss in this book that I haven't done myself, but it stands up well in theory.

Always bear in mind that declaratory judgments do not involve damages of any kind, and only court costs can be recovered, not attorney's fees. If the creditor is reporting falsely and it's impacting you negatively, then you might just consider going for a tort in civil court and attempting to collect punitive damages. Punitive damages are not only relative to the offense, but relative to the total market value of the offending company. In other words, there could be a lot of money involved. If your case is strong enough and the damage egregious enough, you may want to get a crackerjack lawyer and have him take the case on a contingency basis.

But most cases really are small; they involve no punitive damages, and the dollar amount isn't enough to pique an attorney's interest. (I use the term *small* loosely, since a $50 unpaid collection account can get you denied and a $200 erroneous bill can drive you mad.)

In all of your dealings, you should be a stickler for details and putting things in writing. Tracking correspondence is a big part of preparing any winning case and methodically planning ahead for what your next move will be. Your actions will cause reactions; if you've played your cards right, then you'll look reasonable and the other party will look unreasonable. Even a nonresponse by someone to a query would likely be interpreted as unreasonable. Always employ tactics that will get the other party to *tell on themselves*, either through writing or by taping phone conversations (if legal and admissable in your state). What better evidence than their own words and deeds? Or should I say misdeeds?

I like going it alone, particularly on the smaller cases. After all, who knows my case and cares as much as I do? Besides, I prefer to pocket the proceeds if there are any. Of course, we're all busy with our daily lives and often just want someone else who knows what he or she is doing to handle things. But sometimes the situation just won't permit this; the dollars involved aren't conducive to legal representation. In such cases, once you've done it by yourself and have been successful, you'll feel empowered and will not likely be trampled on again.

### Erroneous Billing

Often people will get billed (or overbilled) for products or services they didn't receive, and then, to add insult to injury, will be harassed by bill collectors who are attempting to collect the bogus debt.

As always, try to reason with the party who billed you (in person if possible). If they agree to resolve the issue in a way that you find favorable, get the agreement in writing and make sure that you stipulate removal of bad credit, if any. If the account has been turned over to a collection agency, try to get the matter referred back to the original creditor in accordance with the chapter on dealing with collectors. Of course, if the collection agency has already purchased the debt, then you can't get it referred back.

> **Tip:** If the erroneous billing involves a credit card, you may be in luck. Often, credit card statements will have charges that either don't belong to you, are for a dollar amount greater than you authorized, or are for goods or services you ordered but never received. In such cases, you usually have 30 to 50 days (depending on the bank) from the date of the billing statement to dispute the charge. (This is why the travel industry loves to bill far in advance of travel, since problems will often arise outside of this dispute period, leaving consumers with no

*recourse.) The technique for disputing a charge is known as a charge-back, and consumers are not responsible for items that the merchant cannot substantiate. Your bank will work on your behalf to resolve the issue, and the burden of proof will be on the merchant's bank to back up the charge. Further, once disputed the charge goes in stasis, the charge won't incur interest charges or show up on your bill until the matter is resolved. As always, send your disputes to your bank via certified mail, return receipt requested. If you're outside the time period allowed for a charge-back, then you'll likely need to use a court option to get the issue resolved, especially since the matter often will end up in collections and damage your credit.*

I like the tactic of filing a request for a declaratory judgment in cases of erroneous billing, since it really offers many advantages. First, if you sue first, then a lawsuit can't end up on your credit report, even if the defendant countersues. Second, it puts the party that erroneously billed you on a defensive footing, made even worse by the fact that they may have to spend a great deal of money should they choose to try and defend it. (Smaller creditors, such as doctors and small businesses, are billed by attorneys by the hour in most cases.) Third, most erroneous billing cases are for small dollar amounts (less than $200), so they will go uncontested and you'll win by default.

Once you're billed improperly, the clock is running and you'll face collection action if you don't do something right away. This action will end up on your credit report, and you'll be harmed by it, which is why filing suit immediately after you've attempted to have it resolved amicably (give your negotiations three days) is a good thing—regardless of the dollar amount.

If a collection agency has purchased the debt, it won't cease its collection efforts until you pay. It will jack up your report and ignore any pleas by you to stop what it's doing. You can always file for a declaratory judgment at this stage, but if you've had your credit report harmed, then you'd be better served by filing a civil suit and seeking punitive damages. List both the collection agency and the creditor as defendants in the same suit. In the end, they'll get theirs and you'll get paid. Just make sure you get copies of all your credit reports and all correspondence as evidence.

> **Note:** When you win a judgment, send a copy to the CRAs and demand that they stop reporting the account (not report it as paid but remove it from your file altogether—be explicit in your demand). Also, as a part of your request for relief, ask the judge to order the defendant(s) to remove the bad credit. With standard civil suits (not declaratory), if the creditor is small and you get a monetary award, then they can squirm as you damage their credit with a judgment! Justice is best delivered with the cold taste of irony.

Sometimes you can file suit against a creditor, who will still hand the matter over to a collection agency. Just send the agency a letter demanding that it cease its collection action and attach a copy of the complaint (lawsuit) against the creditor. Inform the agency that it's next if it doesn't comply. This is usually enough, but be prepared to sue the agency as well if it doesn't heed your warning.

### Small Claims Court

Small claims court is an option in some circumstances, although this isn't a place where you can get punitive damages. On the other hand, the rules are far looser, and you aren't frowned upon by the court for not having a lawyer. Simple, easy-to-file forms are provided by the court, and you can take just about any civil issue before a court, so long as the matter occurred in the state in which you are filing. Claims regarding credit sometimes can be heard in small claims court, but only if they meet the monetary cap of that particular state and other conditions are met.

You can't get a declaratory judgment in small claims, since a declaratory judgment requires the plaintiff to be seeking damages. This isn't a problem if you've had something show up in your credit that doesn't belong; you can request damages for that. As always, you have to bring evidence to support your claim, such as the credit report itself and/or a denial letter from a creditor with whom you've applied for credit. Surely the amount of damages is subjective, but ask for whatever you feel is reasonable. In your request for relief, ask for damages, but also request that the judge rule that you were damaged by way of a credit report (and/or erroneously billed if it applies). The creditor will have to stop reporting wrongly, or you can always sue again. If you're in a hurry and need the bad mark taken off immediately, provide a copy of the judgment to the CRAs and demand that they remove the derogatory information.

> **Note:** Most small claims courts have narrow venue guidelines, meaning that the offense has to have occurred in the state where you file, and both parties must reside in that state. (Suing a collection agency based in Idaho when you live in Nebraska doesn't work, even if the offense occurred in Nebraska.) Other civil courts have jurisdiction simply based on where the offense occurred.

Other cases that are commonly heard in small claims include billing/overbilling for services, unlawfully issued checks, traffic accidents, property leases, dog bites, and contract work. The awards in most states consist of a monetary judgment (with a cap based on local law), and other states will permit recovery of property (with a cap). Most have monetary damage limits ranging from $2,000 to $5,000. Check with your local small claims court to see if your case can be heard there.

### Property Leases

A dispute regarding a property lease is another prime candidate for a declaratory judgment request. I'll come back to the pursuit of this legal avenue, but, but first I want to address some ways in which you can greatly enhance your position as a tenant in the event that it comes to that.

The property lease is unique in so many ways, not the least of which is the fact that you have the ability to specify the terms of the contract before signing it, unlike with preprinted contracts from lenders.

Before you sign, you can build in desirable terms, particularly exit terms. Some examples of this are the option to vacate with 60 days notice (even though you signed for a year), with no penalty, the option to sublet, and the option to transfer the lease. Make sure that everything is agreed to in writing, especially pet policies (if you own a pet).

Once you have negotiated your terms and have signed the lease, you have another opportunity to document the condition of the unit and other potential problems. I strongly recommend using a camcorder to take video footage of the premises before you move in. Use a newspaper published from that day in the footage so there are no question marks later, and state in the intro of the video what you are doing and why. If you don't have a camcorder or can't borrow one, then take pictures at the very least. Landlords are notorious for cheating tenants, and these measures are invaluable in terms of protecting yourself.

If for some reason the unit doesn't work out and you need to vacate before the lease expires, give the landlord a call and explain the circumstances. Sometimes a landlord will be glad you're leaving and will let you out of the lease. If the unit didn't live up to your expectations (e.g., barking dog, bad neighbors, landlord's failure to make repairs, and so forth), create a paper trail every time something goes wrong. That is, notify the owner in writing, using the insurance method. This avoids the he said/she said routine.

*Tip: Never abandon a unit; not only will it look bad in front of a judge, but the owner can say anything he*

*or she wants about the condition of the unit and will
likely be believed. After all, if you were a judge, would
you believe someone who just walked with no communication and no notice?*

If the landlord is willing to let you out of the lease, of
course you'll need to get it in writing immediately, with all of
the terms spelled out succinctly. In a case where the owner is
unwilling to let you out or agree to what you deem are reasonable terms, consider whether he lived up to his end of the
contract (e.g., was the property safe, quiet, functional?). You
may need to send a "notice of intent to vacate in 30 days" (30
days is always considered reasonable notice) and request a
reasonable time for a walk-through to be completed and the
keys/garage door openers turned in.

Whether the owner agrees to meet in order to perform a
walk-thru or not, don't argue; have the place professionally
cleaned, including carpets, and keep your receipts. Take more
video (or pictures) on the day of departure, and include the
landlord in the shots if possible.

Even though the landlord may still want a lease penalty, he
may be willing to perform the walk-through and sign a statement saying he received the unit (and the keys) back in a satisfactory condition. Get this if you can. If he's unwilling to do
this or has made himself unavailable, return the keys with a
note explaining what your intentions are and stating that the
keys are enclosed; use the insurance method, as always. What
you're doing is mitigating the damage a paving the way for
what could be a legal battle. (Go to your local courthouse and
ask the clerk what the most common complaint filed is . . . the
answer will be landlord-tenant disputes.)

What are your intentions? Well, that depends on many
factors, like how much the landlord claims you owe, how far
apart you are, whether or not he's being reasonable, and
under what conditions you felt compelled to move in the first
place. Your intentions may be to get out of the lease without
paying any penalties, in spite of the fact that the contract calls

for them, or perhaps to litigate in order to get damages for unnecessary suffering (hard to prove, unless you are totally disabled), or simply to get your deposit back. Some of this may be attainable if you can demonstrate that the landlord didn't live up to his end of the bargain and that you were the reasonable one.

Your first course under adversarial conditions would be to send the notice of intent to vacate and explain the reasons. If you get a response that you're not happy with, stay as amicable as you can and, as stated before, get the owner to sign a statement that he received the unit in good order/received the keys.

> **Tip:** Never lease a unit from a management company or agent of the owner. If you ever have a problem, it will inevitably sink into the abyss, with each party blaming the other. The mess that will ensue will not only drive you mad, but litigation can become problematic due to the convoluted nature of it.

Once you've vacated and still can't obtain a release from the lease, you can get more aggressive. Now you're in a time crunch, as doing nothing will inevitably lead to collection action, likely from a collection agency. *Your credit will surely be damaged if you don't take preemptive action to stop it.*

Before that happens, immediately send a follow-up letter (using the insurance method) stating that you tried to be amicable, but since the landlord is not, you'll take the following actions within 10 days if you don't hear back: a) notify the health department of specific violations (if they exist); b) Notify HUD of the same deficiencies; c) notify the attorney general's office of the same. Is the owner operating under a real estate license? Explain that you'll also notify the state agency that oversees such licenses. Also, if it were me, I'd inform the landlord of my intention to file suit and seek damages, since he failed to live up to his end of the contract. Wait 14 days, and then do whatever you said you were going to do in your letter.

Litigation under landlord-tenant laws can be quite troublesome, which is why many lawyers don't take such cases, and the ones that do want a retainer up front and will only work on an hourly rate (no flat rates). And those hours can add up really fast . . .

Many states have laws stating that "irreparable damage" must have occurred before you can get damages from a landlord, and this standard is usually an insurmountable hurdle. While Americans with Disabilities Act (ADA) cases are the exception, these cases are tricky and are conducted in federal court. You'll need an attorney for sure, one that specializes in such cases. Federal court can be quite complicated (even for attorneys), and new laws are being written on ADA every day. It's the most progressive area of the law in America as of this writing.

Of course, some states have more favorable tenant laws, so it's up to you to learn what you can and/or consult an attorney. Don't assume anything.

Any more, if the dollar amount is high enough, property owners (i.e., their counsel) will simply file suit against you not long after they've attempted collection action. This suit will likely end up on your credit report and damage you immensely. (The collection action itself will damage you as well.) Furthermore, they'll often sue for far more than the contract actually calls for, or for damages that don't exist.

If you are walking out of a lease for good reason (i.e., the owner broke the lease) and the owner won't agree to void the contract, then your best course is to file suit right away, requesting a declaratory judgment.

This works well in many ways. First, if you retain a lawyer and threaten a lawsuit, then they could sue you first; in anticipation of your action. As stated previously, by rule, if *you* are the plaintiff, the lawsuit won't end up on your credit report—even if the other party countersues! If the other party sues you first, then it will likely end up on your credit report.

Keep in mind that a lawsuit on your credit report is not the same as a collection account, which brings me to my second point: even though you've sued first, the landlord can still hand the matter over to a collection agency and attempt to collect the debt, but it's unlikely. The debt will most likely remain with the landlord's in-house or contracted attorney, and it won't show up on your report as a collection action. Now you've potentially saved yourself two bad marks, and maybe even a third (i.e., a judgment, which is what would have happened if you had just run away from it).

Even if the debt is handed over to a collection agency while in litigation, a letter from your attorney demanding that it be removed will almost always lead to removal. The landlord knows you're serious at that point, since you've filed suit once already.

Third, the debt surely can't be sold to a third party when it's in litigation, which is even better.

*These are all compelling reasons why you don't waste too much time with threats—you file suit right when you know there's trouble.*

If collection action has already begun and the landlord hasn't sued you yet, try to settle the matter in accordance with the methods spelled out earlier in the sections on removing information that is negative but true and removing information that is negative but false. Through discussion, find out where the landlord is at with the collection action and get a handle on where it's going. Like I said, you may also consider suing first if you can demonstrate that you've been wronged in some way.

> **Note:** You have the right to the quiet, peaceful enjoyment of the property, safety, and basic services. If any of these conditions were not met, then your landlord is in breach of the lease.

There are so many possible scenarios and circumstances surrounding leases, and tenant-landlord laws vary widely from state to state. Carefully judge your situation, and if you feel that you aren't making any headway on your own, then contact an attorney.

> **Caution:** *With leases, the bottom line is this: you must act fast, before your credit is damaged. It's a pain in the neck, but being proactive will save you a great deal of time and money in the long run.*

## A SAMPLE LAWSUIT AGAINST A COLLECTION AGENCY

As you may already know, either from personal experience or otherwise, collection agencies are the bane of the credit reporting system. Their daily modus operandi is devoid of manners, tact, common decency, and respect for the law. As stated previously, the law itself isn't enough of a deterrent for their hooliganism, but the legal option for handling them can be useful when you find that all other methods have failed.

I once had a bill collector from the collection agency Risk Management Alternatives call me at 7 A.M. (Allowable hours are between 8 A.M. and 9 P.M.) He also called me three times in one day and left messages—not to mention lying. Of course, I told him I would sue, but did he believe me? Of course not—I'm an idiot.

I sued the New Jersey-based collection agency in Oregon State Circuit Court, county of Deschutes (where I lived at the time). I could sue them locally since it was they who called me when I was in Oregon. Had I called them, then I would likely have had to retain a New Jersey attorney, which might have caused me to give it up altogether.) The remedies I requested were attorney fees (I didn't have an attorney, but I had determined that I would go to trial with one if it went that far), court costs, $20,000 in actual damages plus $1,000 in additional damages for violating 15 USC 1692k, a uniform commercial code dealing with collections. (Actual damages are subjective and relative to the amount of grief and hardship inflicted. I used $20,000, since it's best to start high.)

I picked up the book *Represent Yourself in Court—How to Prepare & Try a Winning Case* and read it cover to cover. I also picked up a copy of and read the local court rules from my county's circuit court (many counties' local rules will differ).

Now that I was ready, I first had to find out what type of entity I was dealing with. Was the defendant a corporation, limited liability company (LLC), or something else? I called the New Jersey secretary of state's office to find out, as well as to get the name and contact information for the defendant's "registered agent." Usually an attorney, the agent is the person who is required to receive a copy of the summons.

The New Jersey secretary of state charged me $20 for the information and provided it over the phone once I provided my credit card number. Now I was ready to file.

I typed up the complaint (using the techniques outlined in the book and copies of old cases at the courthouse) and filed it with the court at a cost of $126. (Had the damages been less than $10,000, the cost would have been $80. States differ on how much they charge, and you can call the court to find out what your state charges.) Since the defendant's registered agent had to be served (which meant typing up a summons and mailing it to the sheriff of the county in which the registered agent resided), I called the sheriff's office and asked about the procedure for service. They informed me that I would need to send them a check for $29 and the original plus three copies of the summons. They also told me to include a copy of the court's hearing notice, which the court provided to me (in triplicate) at the time of filing. Many state courts will perform the entire servicing process (referred to as "service") automatically. Check your local county's court rules or ask the clerk of courts.

Once the registered agent was served, the sheriff's office sent me "proof of service" in triplicate. I filed the original with the court, and the defendant had 30 days from the date of service in which to respond to the court. Some crony from the legal department of the defendant called me very shortly thereafter and made an offer of $2,000 to settle. She also claimed that the company didn't normally operate this way and was very apologetic. After taking up her time and throwing a fit for about an hour, I told her I wasn't buying it. I felt that her company was in the business of badgering people, and now it was my turn. I told her that the price was $16,000 if she wanted to settle, explaining that her company would have to retain an Oregon attorney, and those costs alone would be from $12,000 to $15,000 if it went to trial. She told me she would think it over.

The next week I received a copy of the answer from the defendant's newly retained Oregon attorney. "Lord, these people are really stupid," I thought. "They would rather pay an attorney than pay me." (My local attorney that I use for larger cases informed me that this is common, and large companies are morons when it comes to settling these matters.) The moment they lawyered up, they were in for $5,000 to $6,000 right out of the gate. "Why not just make a counteroffer to me of $5,000," I wondered.

Their attorney did one smart thing; he made a formal "offer of judgment" of $2,500. This is a good tactic, since plaintiffs who decline such offers are not entitled to get attorney fees even if they win at trial, if the award is less than the offer of judgment. So, if it had gone to trial, I had won, and the judge had awarded me $2,499, then I would have had to pay my own attorney fees, which can run somewhere in the neighborhood of $10,000 to $15,000. Of course, I could go to trial without an attorney, but that can be risky and I prefer not to, depending on how complicated the case is.

Yet he was not well versed on the local court rules and made two errors. First, he submitted a "demand for jury trial" (the case would be heard by a judge by default unless a plaintiff or defendant submitted such a demand), which was not even possible because my claim didn't meet the dollar requirements in that county for a trial by jury. Second, he didn't know exactly how much time a defendant has to accept a formal offer of judgment. In this case it was three days, and if he had done his homework he would have known this.

After bending his ear for about an hour and wrecking his day, I signed the offer of judgment, made a copy, and filed it with the court. By Oregon law, I had only three days to accept the offer (which truly puts pressure on the plaintiff if the offer is good enough. This one was good enough for me, since many awards are, unfairly, only in the hundreds of dollars.) I then created a "stipulation of judgment," which simply said that as soon as I received $2,500, I would dismiss the case with prejudice. (That means that the case could not be reopened in the future for any reason.) Here is the exact wording I used:

> THIS MATTER coming before the court upon the stipulation of the parties, by and through their respective attorney(s) of record; the court being fully advised herein; now, therefore
>
> IT IS HEREBY ORDERED AND ADJUDGED that defendant will pay plaintiff the sum of $2,500 and plaintiff will, upon receiving the sum, request a dismissal of this case with prejudice.

This was to be signed by me, the defendant's attorney, and then filed with the court. The judge would have to sign it to make it binding. I signed it and sent it to the defendant's attorney for signature. He, in turn, sent me his own version of the Stipulation of Judgment, which read like this:

> Based on defendant's ORCP 54 E Offer of Judgment, which plaintiff has accepted, the parties stipulate that:
>
> A judgment be entered against the defendant in the amount of $2,500, inclusive of all damages, fees, and costs;
> Upon receiving proof of check from defendant in the amount of the stipulated judgment, plaintiff shall execute (a) this stipulated money judgment; and (b) a satisfaction of judgment in the form attached. Upon receiving those exe-

cuted documents from plaintiff, defendant shall (a) send plaintiff the original settlement check, which plaintiff shall be authorized to negotiate; and (b) file the executed documents with the court.

The attorney included a copy of the check made out to me from the defendant, along with another document, a "satisfaction of judgment," which I was required to sign and return with the stipulation.

What's wrong with this picture? Why in the hell would I sign a satisfaction of judgment when it wasn't *really* satisfied? Some people might consider signing this pile of crap and returning it to the defendant, but I am not one of them. I called the attorney and left the following message on his voice mail: "I have received your mail . . . these terms are unacceptable. I will dismiss the case only after I have received payment in full, and that point is nonnegotiable. Feel free to call me and let me know how you want to proceed."

If I signed the satisfaction of judgment, the case would be dismissed. What if they decided not to send me the check? I don't want to know the answer to that question.

What reason could the attorney have for inserting "proof of check" instead of "payment in full"? Smells like nothing but trouble, and in all the many hundreds of old case files I reviewed at the Oregon state courthouse, I had never seen anything like this—or heard of it for that matter. Perhaps the attorney thought I was a neophyte and would bite. Perhaps I am—but this newbie surely wouldn't agree to dismiss anything without the cash in hand.

The attorney called me back and offered to have a local attorney (he was 150 miles away) meet with me to exchange the check/documents, which I accepted. This satisfied both of our needs and put the whole thing back on track. He sent the new stipulation to a local attorney, and I met with that attorney, signed the documents, and was handed the check.

My resource costs totaled $175 plus time, and I received

$2,500. The defendant probably incurred $3,000 to $4,000 in legal fees, which put their total costs at $5,500 to $6,500. Not bad, eh? They got spanked for their hooliganism, and I got a few bucks for my troubles, not to mention a good story for this book.

Of course, I had to pay income tax on the $2,500; the collection agency sent me a 1099 (a copy also goes to the IRS), but still . . . not a bad deal.

Below is a copy of the check and the stub for $2,500, and the final offer of judgment for $2,500 can be found on the following page.

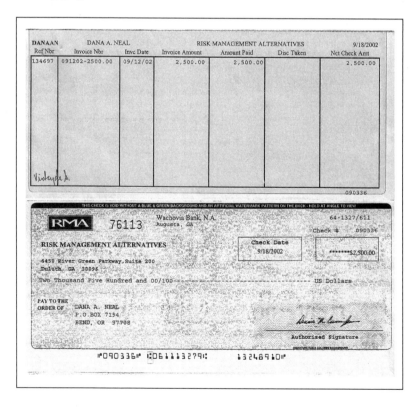

IN THE CIRCUIT COURT OF THE STATE OF OREGON

FOR THE COUNTY OF DESCHUTES

| | |
|---|---|
| DANA A. NEAL, | Case No. 02CV0339AB |
| Plaintiff, | OFFER OF JUDGMENT |
| v. | |
| RISK MANAGEMENT ALTERNATIVES, INC., | |
| Defendant. | |

Pursuant to ORCP 54 E, defendant offers to allow judgment against it in the amount of TWO THOUSAND FIVE HUNDRED Dollars ($2,500), inclusive of all damages, fees and costs.

DATED this 5th day of September, 2002.

COSGRAVE VERGEER KESTER LLP

David H. Williams, OSB #75386
Robert E. Sabido, OSB #96416
Of Attorneys for Defendant

Trial Attorney: David H. Williams

Defendant's offer of judgment is accepted by plaintiff this ___ day of September, 2002.

Dana A. Neal, *pro se*

Page 1 -    OFFER OF JUDGMENT

403901-1

COSGRAVE, VERGEER & KESTER LLP
Attorneys at Law
Bank of America Financial Center
121 SW Morrison • Suite 1300
Portland, Oregon 97204-3193
(503) 323-9000

▲

# CHAPTER 8

# BAD
# TECNIQUES FROM
# SO-CALLED
# EXPERTS

I've read some unusual tactics in popular credit repair books, and as far as I'm concerned, they should almost never be tried. (One exception is restrictively endorsed checks, but only in rare circumstances and for a particular purpose.) The so-called experts have likely never tried what they purport to be correct. Since Iconsider it my duty to be up on all of the latest techniques in my business, I routinely try things out in order to evaluate such claims and determine what's really true and what isn't. Don't do the same, as you are risking your credit and possibly more.

## RESTRICTIVELY
## ENDORSED CHECKS

There are books that tout using restrictively endorsed checks as a way to get out of paying credit card bills. The recommended tactic goes like this:

Send a letter to the creditor that spells out the terms of your proposed settlement, along with a check. On the back of the check, be sure to include the phrase, "This constitutes payment in full for . . . [whatever the goods/services are] due to . . . [our dispute over] . . ." In the memo block on the front of the check, write "Restrictively Endorsed." The amount of the check can be for whatever you feel is reasonable.

If the creditor cashes the check, send the CRAs a copy of the letter you sent the creditor along with a copy of the check (once it has cleared your bank).

The book in which I read about this technique says that CRAs are then required by law to remove the derogatory item from your report. Well, I tried this technique, and the CRAs would not remove the item. In addition, just to be sure, I had my lawyer send them a demand letter, which also did not work. So what good is the use of restrictively endorsed checks for credit repair?

I did some research in order to get to the heart of the law in this type of matter, and basically, it boils down to "accord and satisfaction." That is, when you spell out the terms of your proposed settlement in your written correspondence and on the back of the check, you have an accord with the other party with regard to those terms. Satisfaction of the accord occurs when the check is cashed.

However, there are mitigating factors that come into play from a legal standpoint. First of all, you already have a contract with the creditor to pay the balance as agreed in your original terms and conditions. Second, by rule, restrictively endorsed checks are only applicable if there's a bona fide dispute already in place over the value/price of the goods or services.

But what's a bona fide dispute? It's where the parties disagree on some issue in the contract, and thus the amount of consideration (dollars/services/goods) given by each side is called into question. Of course, the parties can have a dispute that isn't in writing, but those in writing give you more support for a legal case, which is why you should always put your disputes in writing and request a response.

To what extent is a dispute applicable to a dollar figure that is unambiguous? You borrowed a certain amount by use of the credit card, and so the value is pretty much without question. There's another rule called a "legal duty rule," which means that you have an obligation to perform the contract. There's always a possibility that the other party breached the contract, but how is this applicable to credit cards? In some rare, odd cases it could happen, but in the normal course of business it's extremely unlikely. What if everyone did this with their credit card payments? If it held up in court, then everyone would be doing it and creditors wouldn't get paid.

Yet in the case of body work performed on a car, for example, the value of the work relative to the dollar amount charged might be called into question, and this is where a bona fide dispute is far more palpable. Was the work actually completed? Did the work performed actually cause a reduction in value of the car? Did the car sit in the shop for an unreasonable period? Was the contract breached by the other party in some way? Complicating things even further, in some states, like Ohio, there's a rule called "substantial performance," where if a contractor's performance departs from the contract in only minor respects, then the contractor is still entitled to get paid.

Let's say you send the restrictively endorsed check to the party with whom you have a contract dispute and the other party cashes it, yet still continues taking collection action and reporting it to the CRAs. In a case where you have good grounds for your dispute and can substantiate it, the restrictively endorsed check may prove somewhat useful.

If you can demonstrate a bona fide contract dispute over something similar to a property lease, auto repair, contract work, or faulty goods and the other party has actually cashed your restrictively endorsed check, you've just added weight to your case (assuming you've properly employed its use under the law). In fact, with the canceled check in hand you could file suit requesting a "declaratory judgment" and provide all of the supporting evidence, including the original contract, receipts for any payments you've made, correspondence, and a copy of the canceled check. This way, you've either preempted collection action or stopped it and possibly prevented a lawsuit from showing up on your credit report, since you've filed first. (More on that in Chapter 7: Court—A Useful and Viable Option.)

> **Note:** I've stated that the restrictively endorsed check isn't a tool for credit repair, but there may be some exceptions where it could work. For example, if you purchased a car and the dealer financed it, then it didn't perform in a reasonable manner and the dealer refused to properly repair it, you may have a case of questionable value with a creditor. As with many things pertaining to law, the laws applying to restrictively endorsed checks vary from state to state; check your local rules.

## THE BILLING ERROR METHOD

Certainly there are times when you can use the fact that you moved and did not get a bill in your negotiations. However, there is another technique out there that is touted as useful when it does not work at all.

According to another popular credit book, creditors must remove any late history if the consumer requests a billing clarification within 60 days of the lateness. Of course, I tried this, using all available techniques for negotiating with the creditor and a sending a demand letter to the CRAs. The derogatory information remained, and I couldn't get it off with a crow bar. This, of course, was an account in good standing otherwise, so I had no leverage to get the creditor to remove the derogatory item. Funny thing, too; here I had remained in exceptional (flawless) standing with this bank over a six-year period, and all I got when I attempted to get a single 30-day lateness (which occurred due to a billing error) removed was abuse. I would have been better off to go full-on delinquent and then negotiate a settlement of 80 percent of the balance with removal of derogatory credit as part of the terms. Unreal.

## FILE SEGREGATION: CREATING A NEW IDENTITY

Many books tout a method whereby you create a new identity through the use of an employee identification number (EIN). This number is issued by the IRS to businesses and has nine digits, just like your Social Security number. You apply for one by starting a business, and then call the IRS to request the number. Once the EIN has been issued, you go into a bank, open an account, provide the EIN on your application just like you would your Social Security number, and wham—now you have a new identity and fresh credit.

Problem is, it's a felony and you can go to prison if caught. It is a federal crime to make any false statements on a loan or credit application. Why would anyone take such a risk, especially given the fact that there are perfectly legally techniques to repair credit that work just fine?

▲

# CHAPTER 9

# IDENTITY THEFT— PREVENTION AND RECOVERY

Identity theft is the fastest growing crime in America. There's a simple reason for this: it's easy, and it pays. I guess criminals figure, why go through life with their crappy identity when they can just steal someone else's for little more than the cost of dining out? You can get an identity package online, complete with a Social Security number, for about $40.

There are two parts to identity theft—prevention and recovery.

## PREVENTION

Here are some guidelines that will help you prevent identity theft:

- Never leave the carbon copies of your credit card transactions

**135**

lying around, and don't throw them in the trash. Get a shredder; the cost is only about $30.

- Don't leave the registration to your car in your glove compartment. Place it in the trunk or carry it in your purse or wallet.
- If possible, place a lock on your mailbox.
- Get an unlisted phone number.
- Credit card companies will often send you solicitations for preapproved credit cards. If you can't put a lock on your mailbox, you should opt out of these offers. You can do so by calling (888) 567-8688. If you decide not to respond to these offers, be sure to shred the application.
- Check your credit reports often, at least every six months.
- Don't put anything in the trash that has your personal data on it. Shred your phone bills, utility bills, and any other bill or document with personal data on it.
- If you use a computer, use a software firewall in order to provide some measure of intrusion protection. The one I recommend right now is Tiny Personal Firewall, available free of charge for home users at www.tinysoftware.com. Not only will this program provide intrusion detection, but it will also catch programs on your computer trying to call out! "Calling out" refers to the process by which software on your computer sends information about you to other computers on the Internet.
- Frequently (once a week) run spyware detection software on your computer. Spyware programs are nefarious software programs, installed without your knowledge, that call out. The two detection programs I recommend are free: Spybot and Ad-Aware. They're available at http://spybot.safer-networking.de and http://www.lavasoft.de.
- Create a startup password for your computer, so that when it boots up you are prompted for it. This works well for nosy baby-sitters, maids, or anyone who may just happen to break into your home while you're on vacation.
- Password-protect all of your accounts. This means credit cards, checking and savings, gas, electric, land phone, cell

phone, Internet service, cable, direct TV, and so on. Make it clear to these companies that when anyone calls about your account, they are to ask for the password first thing. If they don't prompt you for it every time you call, then make it clear you want to be prompted.

- Never carry your Social Security card around with you (or anything else with your number it on it). Many states will even give you a driver's license without your Social Security number on it if you request it.

- Never give out your SSN to anyone unless absolutely necessary. Even rental car agencies request it, but I'll often ramble off a fake one since it's none of their business.

- Don't give your SSN over the Internet for any reason, except if it's a bank site.

- If you live in California (and possibly other states as well, check your local rules), send a "victim statement letter" to the three CRAs (see Appendix A for a sample). You don't have to be a victim to send it. This will require that the potential lender notify you when someone requests credit extended in your name. There are two down sides to this: 1) you will not be able to get credit approval as quickly as you would otherwise—instant credit will be impossible; 2) you will not be able to get your online credit report. (CRAs often change their numbers and addresses to avoid filing these papers, since it costs them money. Be sure to contact the CRAs to get their current address for filing victim statements, and notify the FTC if there is any monkey business.)

- Send a "Request for Verification Letter" to the Department of Motor Vehicles (DMV). The Driver's Privacy Protection Act (DPPA) was passed in June of 2000. It requires that all state DMVs will close records to the public. This occurred after several well-publicized road-rage incidents, where people were gunned down after raging maniacs simply went to the DMV and, using the victim's license plate number, obtained their address. This Act is a good start, but you can do more to ensure that someone does not attempt to get a driver's license under your name. When you provide a "request for verification letter" to the DMV, it requires that you be notified personally, by phone, or in writing, before a driver's license is issued in your name. Contact your state DMV for more information.

Once identity theft has occurred, you will certainly fight an uphill battle to get things straightened out. That's why it's so important to take these fraud prevention tips seriously so that it never happens to you. Innocent people often go to jail or have judgments against them because of identity theft. Furthermore, if your identity is stolen, the system of credit and finance in this country is not going to be sensitive to your cause. In most cases, you will find them unwilling to help you at all.

## RECOVERY

Here are some things you can do if you become a victim of identity theft:

- File a police report. Send a copy to all three CRAs and creditors—even creditors not yet affected. Use the insurance method, of course.
- Use the FTC form "ID Fraud Affidavit" (available on www.ftc.gov/bcp/conline/pubs/credit/affadavit.pdf) and mail it to all three CRAs. You may also request this form by mail: Federal Trade Commission, CRC-240 Washington, D.C. 20580
- Be prepared to sue companies that spread false information about you. It's now federal law that you have two years from the occurrence to file suit, so don't delay if you've been a victim.

It's also a good idea to log on to www.consumer.gov periodically for the latest updates and changes to the law. You might find something fresh there that may assist you.

# ▲
# SOME FINAL
# THOUGHTS

It's easy to see why the quest for credit improvement can become so complicated. With the lawyers, collectors, the FTC rules, CRAs, state laws, and the spectrum of personalities—it's not hard to see why people just simply run from the problem.

Yet there are some other bright spots, since knowing the rules, having a plan, and taking action will nearly always result in a desirable outcome.

Don't be overwhelmed or intimidated, be steadfast, and don't take no for an answer. Just apply what you've learned and create a credit profile that looks exactly the way you want it.

▲

# SAMPLE LETTERS

*WARNING:* It is very important that you use the letters provided here only as a guide. Never use the exact wording or structure, as doing so may tip the reader that you are using a credit repair technique or program.

**Note:** Remember that CRAs are notorious for stalling and will use whatever means to prevent them from having to do something. The most common delay tactic is to respond to your letter asking you to verify that "you are who you say you are," by resubmitting your request along with a copy of a utility bill that provides verification of your address. They should not require this, but this is not the battle to fight. In your first correspondence, always include a copy of a bill. For those wishing to be "lost," use one that has been sent to your P.O. Box, not to your home address. If you use your home address, it will end up on your credit report and creditors will have found you.

## CEASE COMMUNICATION LETTER—FOR CREDITORS

This letter is for creditors, not collection agencies. Send it when requesting that a creditor stop contacting you.

Always review the appropriate section of this book before sending this or any other letter.

**Use your own words; these words are a guide only.**

[date]


Mr. Homer Hancock
First Bank of Simpsons
555 Ruff Ruff Road
Denzel, WA  00000


RE: First Bank of Simpsons, Acct # 0000 0000 0000 0000

Mr. Hancock:

I request that you cease communication regarding [account #] immediately. I'm familiar with the Fair Debt Collection Practices Act, and you must comply with this request.

Sincerely,


Joe P. Snuffy

## CEASE COMMUNICATION LETTER—
## FOR COLLECTION AGENCIES

This letter is for collection agencies, not creditors. It is to be used when demanding that a collection agency stop contacting you, or when you want the matter referred back to the original creditor. Always review the appropriate section of this book before sending this or any other letter.

**Use your own words; these words are a guide only.**

[date]


Mr. Homer Hellhound
First Collection Agency of Snakes and Worms
555 Cya Later Road
Denzel, WA  00000


RE: [Original Creditor Name], Acct # 0000 0000 0000 0000

Mr. Hellhound:

I demand that you cease communication immediately and refer the matter back to [Original Creditor]. I'm familiar with the Fair Debt Collection Practices Act, and you must comply with this demand.

Sincerely,


Joe P. Snuffy

## DEMAND FOR CRA(S) TO REMOVE INQUIRY

This letter is for credit reporting agencies. It is to be used when requesting that they remove an inquiry from your report. Always review the appropriate section of this book before sending this or any other letter.

**Use your own words; these words are a guide only.**

[date]

[name of CRA]
[address of CRA]
[city, state, Zip of CRA]

RE: Remove Unauthorized Inquiries

[CRA]:

I have recently received a copy of my credit file and noticed that there are unauthorized inquiries on it. This is illegal; as I didn't authorize this, it is a violation of the Fair Credit Reporting Act.
[If you know that the inquiry was supposed to be for a periodic review and not for extension of credit, state it here.]
This transgression has hurt my chances of getting credit and caused me to be denied. I demand that you remove the following inquiries immediately:

[name of creditor]
[date of inquiry]
[subscriber code] (if there is one)

I expect your compliance. If you do comply, I will consider the matter closed and will take no legal action against you. If you do not, I will take legal action.
Consider this is a formal notice. I expect your compliance of my request, as well as a copy of the corrected report provided to me, within 10 days.

Sincerely,

Joe P. Snuffy

## DEMAND FOR CREDITOR TO REMOVE INQUIRY

This letter is for creditors only. It is to be used when requesting that they remove an inquiry from your report.

Always review the appropriate section of this book before sending this or any other letter.

**Use your own words; these words are a guide only.**

---

[date]

[name of creditor]
[address of creditor]
[city, state, Zip of creditor]

RE: Remove Unauthorized Inquiries

[Creditor]:

I have recently received a copy of my credit file and noticed that there is an/are some unauthorized inquiry/inquiries on it. This is illegal; as I didn't authorize this, it is a violation of the Fair Credit Reporting Act.

(If you know that the inquiry was supposed to be for a periodic review and not for extension of credit, state it. Example: "I understand that you have the right for a periodic review of my credit report; however, those inquiries are supposed to be private and not for potential lenders to review, and [name of CRA(s)] lists the inquiry as public.")

This transgression has hurt my chances of getting credit and caused me to be denied. I demand that you remove the following immediately:

[date]

[name of creditor]
[date of inquiry]
[subscriber code] (if there is one)

I expect your compliance. If you do comply, I will consider the matter closed and will take no legal action against you. If you do not, I will take legal action.

Consider this is a formal notice. I expect your compliance, as well as a copy of the corrected report, provided to me within 10 days.

Sincerely,

Joe P. Snuffy

## REQUEST FOR CRA(S) TO REMOVE INFORMATION

This letter is for credit reporting agencies. It is to be used when requesting that derogatory or incorrect information be removed from your report.

Always review the appropriate section of this book before sending this or any other letter.

**Use your own words; these words are a guide only.**

---

[date]


[name of CRA]
[address of CRA]
[city, state, Zip of CRA]


RE: Reporting of Creditor Information (Name, Acct #)

[CRA]:

I request that you remove any negative credit information regarding (creditor name), account # [account number]. The information you are reporting is false, and in accordance with the Fair Credit Reporting Act, you are not permitted to report false information.

This is a formal notice, and I expect your compliance of my request, as well as a copy of the corrected report provided to me, within 10 days.


Thank you for your consideration.


Sincerely,


Joe P. Snuffy

## DEMAND FOR CRA(S) TO REMOVE INFORMATION

This letter is for credit reporting agencies. It is for use when demanding that derogatory or incorrect information be removed.

Always review the appropriate section before sending this or any other letter.

**Use your own words; these words are a guide only.**

---

[date]


[name of CRA]
[address of CRA]
[city, state, Zip of CRA]

RE: Reporting of Creditor Information (Name, Acct #)

[CRA]:

On [date], I sent you a letter requesting that you remove any negative credit information regarding [creditor name], account # [account number]. The information you are reporting is false, and in accordance with the Fair Credit Reporting Act, you are not permitted to report false information.

Your continued negligence has caused me harm, since it has affected my ability to [specify the harm it has caused]. The information you are reporting is false because [reason].

You have failed to comply with my request, and you may now consider it a demand. This is a formal notice, and I expect your compliance, as well as a copy of the corrected report provided to me, within 10 days. If you fail to do so, I will take legal action against you.

Sincerely,


Joe P. Snuffy

## VICTIM STATEMENT LETTER

You don't have to be a victim to send this letter. This will require that a potential lender notify you when someone requests credit extended in your name. There are two downsides to this: 1) You will not be able to get credit approval as quickly as you would otherwise; instant credit will be impossible, and 2) You will not be able to get your online credit report. (CRAs often change their numbers and addresses to avoid filing these papers, since it costs them money. Be sure to contact the CRAs to get their current address for filing victim statements, and notify the FTC if there is any monkey business.)

[date]

[name of CRA]
Fraud Unit Department
[address]
[city, state, Zip]

RE: Victim Statement Letter

To whom it may concern:

Since fraudulent applications may be submitted in my name using accurate personal information, please verify with me that applications for credit are legitimate.

Last Name:
First Name:
Middle Initial:
Social Security Number:
Date of Birth:
Driver's License Number:
Street Number:
City:
State:
Zip:
Former Address:
Day Phone:
Evening Phone:

I've enclosed a copy of my [insert type of document that was formerly addressed to you at the address listed above, e.g. utility bill, etc.] for verification of my identity.

Thank you for your attention in this matter.

Sincerely,


Joe P. Snuffy

▲

# DEFINITIONS

**acct clsd/grantors req**—Creditor canceled charge privileges.

**bankruptcy**—A filed and discharged bankruptcy.

**bk liq reo**—Account written off in bankruptcy.

**charge-off**—Creditor has written the debt off, assuming that it is not collectible. Creditors often will sell the debt to a third party at a discount, i.e., send it to a collection agency. The creditor can get tax credit for charge-offs.

**collection account**—Creditor has given up on collecting and has sold the debt to a third party (collection agency).

**CRA**—Credit reporting agency.

**creditor**—One who loans money.

**current account**—All payments to date have been on time.

**current was 60/90**—Late both 60 and 90 days. How many times each will accompany this on a report.

**debtor**—One that owes money to a creditor.

**delinquent**—Past due.

**inc in bk**—Account written off in bankruptcy. Must have a $0 balance.

**insurance method**—Always use this method when dealing with creditors and credit reporting agencies: all promises are made in writing and spelled out. All correspondence via mail is sent to creditors using certified mail, return receipt requested.

**judgment**—Someone has taken you to court and wins the suit.

**paid as agreed**—Loan paid on time.

**paid charge-off**—Charged-off account that was eventually paid; often a ploy by the creditor to get you to pay in exchange for this rating. Better than a charge-off, but still negative.

**paid collection**—Same as paid charge-off but done by a collection agency instead of a creditor.

**paid satisfactory**—Loan paid in accordance with terms.

**paid was 60/90/120**—Paid, but not until it was 60, 90, or 120 days late.

**refinanced**—Borrowed additional money from the same creditor, combining the first loan with the second.

**repossession**—An item used as collateral for the loan was taken back by the creditor.

**settled**—Usually means debtor owed more than creditor settled for.

**Scnl**—Subscriber cannot locate. Debtor has skipped and failed to pay.

**secured credit card**—A credit card that requires a cash balance in an account. The cash balance is usually also the credit card limit.

**tax lien**—Usually reported for back taxes owed, associated with property.

**unrated**—The rating isn't negative or positive, but neutral.

usually reported as I0, R0, or UR (installment unrated, revolving unrated, or simply unrated.) It can be negative if looked at by human eyes, but doesn't affect a credit score.

**written off in bk**—Debt removed due to bankruptcy, requires a zero balance.

▲

# THE FAIR CREDIT REPORTING ACT

As a public service, the staff of the Federal Trade Commission (FTC) has prepared the following complete text of the Fair Credit Reporting Act (FCRA), 15 U.S.C. § 1681 et seq. Although staff generally followed the format of the U.S. Code as published by the Government Printing Office, the format of this text does differ in minor ways from the Code (and from West's U.S. Code Annotated). For example, this version uses FCRA section numbers (§§ 601-625) in the headings. (The relevant U.S. Code citation is included with each section heading and each reference to the FCRA in the text.)

This version of the FCRA is complete as of July 1999. It includes the amendments to the FCRA set forth in the Consumer Credit Reporting Reform Act of 1996 (Public Law 104-208, the Omnibus Consolidated Appropriations Act for Fiscal Year 1997, Title II, Subtitle D, Chapter 1), Section 311 of the Intelligence Authorization for Fiscal Year 1998 (Public Law 105-107), and the Consumer Reporting Employment Clarification Act of 1998 (Public Law 105-347).

## TABLE OF CONTENTS

§ 601. Short title

This title may be cited as the Fair Credit Reporting Act.

§ 602. Congressional findings and statement of purpose [15 U.S.C. § 1681]

(a) Accuracy and fairness of credit reporting. The Congress makes the following findings:

(1) The banking system is dependent upon fair and accurate credit reporting. Inaccurate credit reports directly impair the efficiency of the banking system, and unfair credit reporting methods undermine the public confidence which is essential to the continued functioning of the banking system.

(2) An elaborate mechanism has been developed for investigating and evaluating the credit worthiness, credit standing, credit capacity, character, and general reputation of consumers.

(3) Consumer reporting agencies have assumed a vital role in assembling and evaluating consumer credit and other information on consumers.

(4) There is a need to insure that consumer reporting agencies exercise their grave responsibilities with fairness, impartiality, and a respect for the consumer's right to privacy.

(b) Reasonable procedures. It is the purpose of this title to require that consumer reporting agencies adopt reasonable procedures for meeting the needs of commerce for consumer credit, personnel, insurance, and other information in a manner which is fair and equitable to the consumer, with regard to the confidentiality, accuracy, relevancy, and proper utilization of such information in accordance with the requirements of this title.

§ 603. Definitions; rules of construction [15 U.S.C. § 1681a]

(a) Definitions and rules of construction set forth in this section are applicable for the purposes of this title.

(b) The term "person" means any individual, partnership, corporation, trust, estate, cooperative, association, government or governmental subdivision or agency, or other entity.

(c) The term "consumer" means an individual.

(d) Consumer report.

(1) In general. The term "consumer report" means any written, oral, or other communication of any information by a consumer reporting agency bearing on a consumer's credit worthiness, credit standing, credit capacity, character, general reputation, personal characteristics, or mode of living which is used or expected to be used or collected in whole or in part for the purpose of serving as a factor in establishing the consumer's eligibility for

(A) credit or insurance to be used primarily for personal, family, or household purposes;

(B) employment purposes; or

(C) any other purpose authorized under section 604 [§ 1681b].

(2) Exclusions. The term "consumer report" does not include

(A) any

(i) report containing information solely as to transactions or experiences between the consumer and the person making the report;

(ii) communication of that information among persons related by common ownership or affiliated by corporate control; or

(iii) communication of other information among persons related by common ownership or affiliated by corporate control, if it is clearly and conspicuously disclosed to the consumer that the information may be communicated among such persons and the consumer is given the opportunity, before the time that the information is initially communicated, to direct that such information not be communicated among such persons;

(B) any authorization or approval of a specific extension of credit directly or indirectly by the issuer of a credit card or similar device;

(C) any report in which a person who has been requested by a third party to make a specific extension of credit directly or indirectly to a consumer conveys his or her decision with respect to such request, if the third party advises the consumer of the name and address of the person to whom the request was made, and such person makes the disclosures to the consumer required under section 615 [§ 1681m]; or

(D) a communication described in subsection (o).

(e) The term "investigative consumer report" means a consumer report or portion thereof in which information on a consumer's character, general reputation, personal characteristics, or mode of living is obtained through personal interviews with neighbors, friends, or associates of the consumer reported on or with others with whom he is acquainted or who may have knowledge concerning any such items of information. However, such information shall not include specific factual information on a consumer's credit record obtained directly from a creditor of the consumer or from a consumer reporting agency when such information was obtained directly from a creditor of the consumer or from the consumer.

(f) The term "consumer reporting agency" means any person which, for monetary fees, dues, or on a cooperative nonprofit basis, regularly engages in whole or in part in the practice of assembling or evaluating consumer credit information or other information on consumers for the purpose of furnishing consumer reports to third parties, and which uses any means or facility of interstate commerce for the purpose of preparing or furnishing consumer reports.

(g) The term "file," when used in connection with information on any consumer, means all of the information on that consumer recorded and retained by a consumer reporting agency regardless of how the information is stored.

(h) The term "employment purposes" when used in connection with a consumer report means a report used for the purpose of evaluating a consumer for employment, promotion, reassignment or retention as an employee.

(i) The term "medical information" means information or records obtained, with the consent of the individual to whom it relates, from licensed physicians or medical practitioners, hospitals, clinics, or other medical or medically related facilities.

(j) Definitions relating to child support obligations.

(1) Overdue support. The term "overdue support" has the meaning given to such term in section 666(e) of title 42 [Social Security Act, 42 U.S.C. § 666(e)].

(2) State or local child support enforcement agency. The term "State or local child support enforcement agency" means a State or local agency which administers a State or local program for establishing and enforcing child support obligations.

(k) Adverse action.

(1) Actions included. The term "adverse action"

(A) has the same meaning as in section 701(d)(6) of the Equal Credit Opportunity Act; and

(B) means

(i) a denial or cancellation of, an increase in any charge for, or a reduction or other adverse or unfavorable change in the terms of coverage or amount of, any insurance, existing or applied for, in connection with the underwriting of insurance;

(ii) a denial of employment or any other decision for employment purposes that adversely affects any current or prospective employee;

(iii) a denial or cancellation of, an increase in any charge for, or any other adverse or unfavorable change in the terms of, any license or benefit described in section 604(a)(3)(D) [§ 1681b]; and

(iv) an action taken or determination that is

(I) made in connection with an application that was made by, or a transaction that was initiated by, any consumer, or in connection with a review of an account under section 604(a)(3)(F)(ii)[§ 1681b]; and

(II) adverse to the interests of the consumer.

(2) Applicable findings, decisions, commentary, and orders. For purposes of any determination of whether an action is an adverse action under paragraph (1)(A), all appropriate final findings, decisions, commentary, and orders issued under section 701(d)(6) of the Equal Credit Opportunity Act by the Board of Governors of the Federal Reserve System or any court shall apply.

(l) Firm offer of credit or insurance. The term "firm offer of credit or insurance" means any offer of credit or insurance to a consumer that will be honored if the consumer is determined, based on information in a consumer report on the consumer, to meet the specific criteria used to select the consumer for the offer, except that the offer may be further conditioned on one or more of the following:

(1) The consumer being determined, based on information in the consumer's application for the credit or insurance, to meet specific criteria bearing on credit worthiness or insurability, as applicable, that are established

(A) before selection of the consumer for the offer; and

(B) for the purpose of determining whether to extend credit or insurance pursuant to the offer.

(2) Verification

(A) that the consumer continues to meet the specific criteria used to select the consumer for the offer, by using information in a consumer report on the consumer, information in the consumer's application for the credit or insurance, or other information bearing on the credit worthiness or insurability of the consumer; or

(B) of the information in the consumer's application for the credit or insurance, to determine that the consumer meets the specific criteria bearing on credit worthiness or insurability.

(3) The consumer furnishing any collateral that is a requirement for the extension of the credit or insurance that was

(A) established before selection of the consumer for the offer of credit or insurance; and

(B) disclosed to the consumer in the offer of credit or insurance.

(m) Credit or insurance transaction that is not initiated by the consumer. The term "credit or insurance transaction that is not initiated by the consumer" does not include the use of a consumer report by a person with which the consumer has an account or insurance policy, for purposes of

(1) reviewing the account or insurance policy; or

(2) collecting the account.

(n) State. The term "State" means any State, the Commonwealth of Puerto Rico, the District of Columbia, and any territory or possession of the United States.

(o) Excluded communications. A communication is described in this subsection if it is a communication

(1) that, but for subsection (d)(2)(D), would be an investigative consumer report;

(2) that is made to a prospective employer for the purpose of

(A) procuring an employee for the employer; or
(B) procuring an opportunity for a natural person to work for the employer;

(3) that is made by a person who regularly performs such procurement;

(4) that is not used by any person for any purpose other than a purpose described in subparagraph (A) or (B) of paragraph (2); and

(5) with respect to which

(A) the consumer who is the subject of the communication

(i) consents orally or in writing to the nature and scope of the communication, before the collection of any information for the purpose of making the communication;

(ii) consents orally or in writing to the making of the communication to a prospective employer, before the making of the communication; and

(iii) in the case of consent under clause (i) or (ii) given orally, is provided written confirmation of that consent by the person making the communication, not later than 3 business days after the receipt of the consent by that person;

(B) the person who makes the communication does not, for the purpose of making the communication, make any inquiry that if made by a prospective employer of the consumer who is the subject of the communication would violate any applicable Federal or State equal employment opportunity law or regulation; and

(C) the person who makes the communication

(i) discloses in writing to the consumer who is the subject of the communication, not later than 5 business days after receiving any request from the consumer for such disclosure, the nature and substance of all information in the consumer's file at the time of the request, except that the sources of any information that is acquired solely for use in making the communication and is actually used for no other purpose, need not be disclosed other than under appropriate discovery procedures in any court of competent jurisdiction in which an action is brought; and

(ii) notifies the consumer who is the subject of the communication, in writing, of the consumer's right to request the information described in clause (i).

(p) Consumer reporting agency that compiles and maintains files on consumers on a nationwide basis. The term "consumer reporting agency that compiles and maintains files on consumers on a nationwide basis" means a consumer reporting agency that regularly engages in the practice of assembling or evaluating, and maintaining, for the purpose of furnishing consumer reports to third parties bearing on a consumer's credit worthiness, credit standing, or credit capacity, each of the following regarding consumers residing nationwide:

(1) Public record information.

(2) Credit account information from persons who furnish that information regularly and in the ordinary course of business.

§ 604. Permissible purposes of consumer reports [15 U.S.C. § 1681b]

(a) In general. Subject to subsection (c), any consumer reporting agency may furnish a consumer report under the following circumstances and no other:

(1) In response to the order of a court having jurisdiction to issue such an order, or a subpoena issued in connection with proceedings before a Federal grand jury.

(2) In accordance with the written instructions of the consumer to whom it relates.

(3) To a person which it has reason to believe

(A) intends to use the information in connection with a credit transaction involving the consumer on whom the information is to be furnished and involving the extension of credit to, or review or collection of an account of, the consumer; or

(B) intends to use the information for employment purposes; or

(C) intends to use the information in connection with the underwriting of insurance involving the consumer; or

(D) intends to use the information in connection with a determination of the consumer's eligibility for a license or other benefit granted by a governmental instrumentality required by law to consider an applicant's financial responsibility or status; or

(E) intends to use the information, as a potential investor or servicer, or current insurer, in connection with a valuation of, or an assessment of the credit or prepayment risks associated with, an existing credit obligation; or

(F) otherwise has a legitimate business need for the information

(i) in connection with a business transaction that is initiated by the consumer; or

(ii) to review an account to determine whether the consumer continues to meet the terms of the account.

(4) In response to a request by the head of a State or local child support enforcement agency (or a State or local government official authorized by the head of such an agency), if the person making the request certifies to the consumer reporting agency that

(A) the consumer report is needed for the purpose of establishing an individual's capacity to make child support payments or determining the appropriate level of such payments;

(B) the paternity of the consumer for the child to which the obligation relates has been established or acknowledged by the consumer in accordance with State laws under which the obligation arises (if required by those laws);

(C) the person has provided at least 10 days' prior notice to the consumer whose report is requested, by certified or registered mail to the last known address of the consumer, that the report will be requested; and

(D) the consumer report will be kept confidential, will be used solely for a purpose described in subparagraph (A), and will not be used in connection with any other civil, administrative, or criminal proceeding, or for any other purpose.

(5) To an agency administering a State plan under Section 454 of the Social Security Act (42 U.S.C. § 654) for use to set an initial or modified child support award.

(b) Conditions for furnishing and using consumer reports for employment purposes.

(1) Certification from user. A consumer reporting agency may furnish a consumer report for employment purposes only if

(A) the person who obtains such report from the agency certifies to the agency that

(i) the person has complied with paragraph (2) with respect to the consumer report, and the person will comply with paragraph (3) with respect to the consumer report if paragraph (3) becomes applicable; and

(ii) information from the consumer report will not be used in violation of any applicable Federal or State equal employment opportunity law or regulation; and

(B) the consumer reporting agency provides with the report, or has previously provided, a summary of the consumer's rights under this title, as prescribed by the Federal Trade Commission under section 609(c)(3) [§ 1681g].

(2) Disclosure to consumer.

(A) In general. Except as provided in subparagraph (B), a person may not procure a consumer report, or cause a consumer report to be procured, for employment purposes with respect to any consumer, unless—

(i) a clear and conspicuous disclosure has been made in writing to the consumer at any time before the report is procured or caused to be procured, in a document that consists solely of the disclosure, that a consumer report may be obtained for employment purposes; and

(ii) the consumer has authorized in writing (which authorization may be made on the document referred to in clause (i)) the procurement of the report by that person.

(B) Application by mail, telephone, computer, or other similar means. If a consumer described in subparagraph (C) applies for employment by mail, telephone, computer, or other similar means, at any time before a consumer report is procured or caused to be procured in connection with that application—

(i) the person who procures the consumer report on the consumer for employment purposes shall provide to the consumer, by oral, written, or electronic means, notice that a consumer report may be obtained for employment purposes, and a summary of the consumer's rights under section 615(a)(3); and

(ii) the consumer shall have consented, orally, in writing, or electronically to the procurement of the report by that person.

(C) Scope. Subparagraph (B) shall apply to a person procuring a consumer report on a consumer in connection with the consumer's application for employment only if—

(i) the consumer is applying for a position over which the Secretary of Transportation has the power to establish qualifications and maximum hours of service pursuant to the provisions of section 31502 of title 49, or a position subject to safety regulation by a State transportation agency; and

(ii) as of the time at which the person procures the report or causes the report to be procured the only interaction between the consumer and the person in connection with that employment application has been by mail, telephone, computer, or other similar means.

(3) Conditions on use for adverse actions.

(A) In general. Except as provided in subparagraph (B), in using a consumer report for employment purposes, before taking any adverse action based in whole or in part on the report, the person intending to take such adverse action shall provide to the consumer to whom the report relates—

(i) a copy of the report; and

(ii) a description in writing of the rights of the consumer under this title, as prescribed by the Federal Trade Commission under section 609(c)(3).

(B) Application by mail, telephone, computer, or other similar means.

(i) If a consumer described in subparagraph (C) applies for employment by mail, telephone, computer, or other similar means, and if a person who has procured a consumer report on the consumer for employment purposes takes adverse action on the employment application based in whole or in part on the report, then the person must provide to the consumer to whom the report relates, in lieu of the notices required under subparagraph (A) of this section and under section 615(a), within 3 business days of taking such action, an oral, written or electronic notification—

(I) that adverse action has been taken based in whole or in part on a consumer report received from a consumer reporting agency;

(II) of the name, address and telephone number of the consumer reporting agency that furnished the consumer report (including a toll-free telephone number established by the agency if the agency compiles and maintains files on consumers on a nationwide basis);

(III) that the consumer reporting agency did not make the decision to take the adverse action and is unable to provide to the consumer the specific reasons why the adverse action was taken; and

(IV) that the consumer may, upon providing proper identification, request a free copy of a report and may dispute with the consumer reporting agency the accuracy or completeness of any information in a report.

(ii) If, under clause (B)(i)(IV), the consumer requests a copy of a consumer report from the person who procured the report, then, within 3 business days of receiving the consumer's request, together with proper identification, the person must send or provide to the consumer a copy of a report and a copy of the consumer's rights as prescribed by the Federal Trade Commission under section 609(c)(3).

(C) Scope. Subparagraph (B) shall apply to a person procuring a consumer report on a consumer in connection with the consumer's application for employment only if—

(i) the consumer is applying for a position over which the Secretary of Transportation has the power to establish qualifications and maximum hours of service pursuant to the provisions of section 31502 of title 49, or a position subject to safety regulation by a State transportation agency; and

(ii) as of the time at which the person procures the report or causes the report to be procured the only interaction between the consumer and the person in connection with that employment application has been by mail, telephone, computer, or other similar means.

(4) Exception for national security investigations.

(A) In general. In the case of an agency or department of the United States Government which seeks to obtain and use a consumer report for employment purposes, paragraph (3) shall not apply to any adverse action by such agency or department which is based in part on such consumer report, if the head of such agency or department makes a written finding that—

(i) the consumer report is relevant to a national security investigation of such agency or department;

(ii) the investigation is within the jurisdiction of such agency or department;

(iii) there is reason to believe that compliance with paragraph (3) will—

(I) endanger the life or physical safety of any person;

(II) result in flight from prosecution;

(III) result in the destruction of, or tampering with, evidence relevant to the investigation;

(IV) result in the intimidation of a potential witness relevant to the investigation;

(V) result in the compromise of classified information; or

(VI) otherwise seriously jeopardize or unduly delay the investigation or another official proceeding.

(B) Notification of consumer upon conclusion of investigation. Upon the conclusion of a national security investigation described in subparagraph (A), or upon the determination that the exception under subparagraph (A) is no longer required for the reasons set forth in such subparagraph, the official exercising the authority in such subparagraph shall provide to the consumer who is the subject of the consumer report with regard to which such finding was made—

(i) a copy of such consumer report with any classified information redacted as necessary;

(ii) notice of any adverse action which is based, in part, on the consumer report; and

(iii) the identification with reasonable specificity of the nature of the investigation for which the consumer report was sought.

(C) Delegation by head of agency or department. For purposes of subparagraphs (A) and (B), the head of any agency or department of the United States Government may delegate his or her authorities under this paragraph to an official of such agency or department who has personnel security responsibilities and is a member of the Senior Executive Service or equivalent civilian or military rank.

(D) Report to the Congress. Not later than January 31 of each year, the head of each agency and department of the United States Government that exercised authority under this paragraph during the preceding year shall submit a report to the Congress on the number of times the department or agency exercised such authority during the year.

(E) Definitions. For purposes of this paragraph, the following definitions shall apply:

(i) Classified information. The term "classified information" means information that is protected from unauthorized disclosure under Executive Order No. 12958 or successor orders.

(ii) National security investigation. The term "national security investigation"means any official inquiry by an agency or department of the United States Government to determine the eligibility of a consumer to receive access or continued access to classified information or to determine whether classified information has been lost or compromised.

(c) Furnishing reports in connection with credit or insurance transactions that are not initiated by the consumer.

(1) In general. A consumer reporting agency may furnish a consumer report relating to any consumer pursuant to subparagraph (A) or (C) of subsection (a)(3) in connection with any credit or insurance transaction that is not initiated by the consumer only if

(A) the consumer authorizes the agency to provide such report to such person; or

(B) (i) the transaction consists of a firm offer of credit or insurance;

(ii) the consumer reporting agency has complied with subsection (e); and

(iii) there is not in effect an election by the consumer, made in accordance with subsection (e), to have the consumer's name and address excluded from lists of names provided by the agency pursuant to this paragraph.

(2) Limits on information received under paragraph (1)(B). A person may receive pursuant to paragraph (1)(B) only

(A) the name and address of a consumer;

(B) an identifier that is not unique to the consumer and that is used by the person solely for the purpose of verifying the identity of the consumer; and

(C) other information pertaining to a consumer that does not identify the relationship or experience of the consumer with respect to a particular creditor or other entity.

(3) Information regarding inquiries. Except as provided in section 609(a)(5) [§ 1681g], a consumer reporting agency shall not furnish to any person a record of inquiries in connection with a credit or insurance transaction that is not initiated by a consumer.

(d) Reserved.

(e) Election of consumer to be excluded from lists.

(1) In general. A consumer may elect to have the consumer's name and address excluded from any list provided by a consumer reporting agency under subsection (c)(1)(B) in connection with a credit or insurance transaction that is not initiated by the consumer, by notifying the agency in accordance with paragraph (2) that the consumer does not consent to any use of a consumer report relating to the consumer in connection with any credit or insurance transaction that is not initiated by the consumer.

(2) Manner of notification. A consumer shall notify a consumer reporting agency under paragraph (1)

(A) through the notification system maintained by the agency under paragraph (5); or

(B) by submitting to the agency a signed notice of election form issued by the agency for purposes of this subparagraph.

(3) Response of agency after notification through system. Upon receipt of notification of the election of a consumer under paragraph (1) through the notification system maintained by the agency under paragraph (5), a consumer reporting agency shall

(A) inform the consumer that the election is effective only for the 2-year period following the election if the consumer does not submit to the agency a signed notice of election form issued by the agency for purposes of paragraph (2)(B); and

(B) provide to the consumer a notice of election form, if requested by the consumer, not later than 5 business days after receipt of the notification of the election through the system established under paragraph (5), in the case of a request made at the time the consumer provides notification through the system.

(4) Effectiveness of election. An election of a consumer under paragraph (1)

(A) shall be effective with respect to a consumer reporting agency beginning 5 business days after the date on which the consumer notifies the agency in accordance with paragraph (2);

(B) shall be effective with respect to a consumer reporting agency

(i) subject to subparagraph (C), during the 2-year period beginning 5 business days after the date on which the consumer notifies the agency of the election, in the case of an election for which a consumer notifies the agency only in accordance with paragraph (2)(A); or

(ii) until the consumer notifies the agency under subparagraph (C), in the case of an election for which a consumer notifies the agency in accordance with paragraph (2)(B);

(C) shall not be effective after the date on which the consumer notifies the agency, through the notification system established by the agency under paragraph (5), that the election is no longer effective; and

(D) shall be effective with respect to each affiliate of the agency.

(5) Notification system.

(A) In general. Each consumer reporting agency that, under subsection (c)(1)(B), furnishes a consumer report in connection with a credit or insurance transaction that is not initiated by a consumer, shall

(i) establish and maintain a notification system, including a toll-free telephone number, which permits any consumer whose consumer report is maintained by the agency to notify the agency, with appropriate identification, of the consumer's election to have the consumer's name and address excluded from any such list of names and addresses provided by the agency for such a transaction; and

(ii) publish by not later than 365 days after the date of enactment of the Consumer Credit Reporting Reform Act of 1996, and not less than annually thereafter, in a publication of general circulation in the area served by the agency

(I) a notification that information in consumer files maintained by the agency may be used in connection with such transactions; and

(II) the address and toll-free telephone number for consumers to use to notify the agency of the consumer's election under clause (I).

(B) Establishment and maintenance as compliance. Establishment and maintenance of a notification system (including a toll-free telephone number) and publication by a consumer reporting agency on the agency's own behalf and on behalf of any of its affiliates in accordance with this paragraph is deemed to be compliance with this paragraph by each of those affiliates.

(6) Notification system by agencies that operate nationwide. Each consumer reporting agency that compiles and maintains files on consumers on a nationwide basis shall establish and maintain a notification system for purposes of paragraph (5)

jointly with other such consumer reporting agencies.

(f) Certain use or obtaining of information prohibited. A person shall not use or obtain a consumer report for any purpose unless

(1) the consumer report is obtained for a purpose for which the consumer report is authorized to be furnished under this section; and

(2) the purpose is certified in accordance with section 607 [§ 1681e] by a prospective user of the report through a general or specific certification.

(g) Furnishing reports containing medical information. A consumer reporting agency shall not furnish for employment purposes, or in connection with a credit or insurance transaction, a consumer report that contains medical information about a consumer, unless the consumer consents to the furnishing of the report.

§ 605. Requirements relating to information contained in consumer reports [15 U.S.C. § 1681c]

(a) Information excluded from consumer reports. Except as authorized under subsection (b) of this section, no consumer reporting agency may make any consumer report containing any of the following items of information:

(1) Cases under title 11 [United States Code] or under the Bankruptcy Act that, from the date of entry of the order for relief or the date of adjudication, as the case may be, antedate the report by more than 10 years.

(2) Civil suits, civil judgments, and records of arrest that from date of entry, antedate the report by more than seven years or until the governing statute of limitations has expired, whichever is the longer period.

(3) Paid tax liens which, from date of payment, antedate the report by more than seven years.

(4) Accounts placed for collection or charged to profit and loss which antedate the report by more than seven years.[1]

(5) Any other adverse item of information, other than records of convictions of crimes which antedates the report by more than seven years.[1]

(b) Exempted cases. The provisions of subsection (a) of this section are not applicable in the case of any consumer credit report to be used in connection with

(1) a credit transaction involving, or which may reasonably be expected to involve, a principal amount of $150,000 or more;

(2) the underwriting of life insurance involving, or which may reasonably be expected to involve, a face amount of $150,000 or more; or

(3) the employment of any individual at an annual salary which equals, or which may reasonably be expected to equal $75,000, or more.

(c) Running of reporting period.

(1) In general. The 7-year period referred to in paragraphs (4) and (6) ** of subsection (a) shall begin, with respect to any delinquent account that is placed for collection (internally or by referral to a third party, whichever is earlier), charged to profit and loss, or subjected to any similar action, upon the expiration of the 180-day period beginning on the date of the commencement of the delinquency which immediately preceded the collection activity, charge to profit and loss, or similar action.

(2) Effective date. Paragraph (1) shall apply only to items of information added to the file of a consumer on or after the date that is 455 days after the date of enactment of the Consumer Credit Reporting Reform Act of 1996.

(d) Information required to be disclosed. Any consumer reporting agency that furnishes a consumer report that contains information regarding any case involving the consumer that arises under title 11, United States Code, shall include in the report an identification of the chapter of such title 11 under which such case arises if provided by the source of the information. If any case arising or filed under title 11, United States Code, is withdrawn by the consumer before a final judgment, the consumer reporting agency shall include in the report that such case or filing was withdrawn upon receipt of documentation certifying such withdrawal.

(e) Indication of closure of account by consumer. If a consumer reporting agency is notified pursuant to section 623(a)(4) [§ 1681s-2] that a credit account of a consumer was voluntarily closed by the consumer, the agency shall indicate that fact in any consumer report that includes information related to the account.

(f) Indication of dispute by consumer. If a consumer reporting agency is notified pursuant to section 623(a)(3) [§ 1681s-2] that information regarding a consumer who was furnished to the agency is disputed by the consumer, the agency shall indicate that fact in each consumer report that includes the disputed information.

§ 606. Disclosure of investigative consumer reports [15 U.S.C. § 1681d]

(a) Disclosure of fact of preparation. A person may not procure or cause to be prepared an investigative consumer report on any consumer unless

(1) it is clearly and accurately disclosed to the consumer that an investigative consumer report including information as to his character, general reputation, personal characteristics and mode of living, whichever are applicable, may be made, and such disclosure

(A) is made in a writing mailed, or otherwise delivered, to the consumer, not later than three days after the date on which the report was first requested, and

(B) includes a statement informing the consumer of his right to request the additional disclosures provided for under subsection (b) of this section and the written summary of the rights of the consumer prepared pursuant to section 609(c) [§ 1681g]; and

(2) the person certifies or has certified to the consumer reporting agency that

(A) the person has made the disclosures to the consumer required by paragraph (1); and

(B) the person will comply with subsection (b).

(b) Disclosure on request of nature and scope of investigation. Any person who procures or causes to be prepared an investigative consumer report on any consumer shall, upon written request made by the consumer within a reasonable period of time after the receipt by him of the disclosure required by subsection (a)(1) of this section, make a complete and accurate disclosure of the nature and scope of the investigation requested. This disclosure shall be made in a writing mailed, or otherwise delivered, to the consumer not later than five days after the date on which the request for such disclosure was received from the consumer or such report was first requested, whichever is the later.

(c) Limitation on liability upon showing of reasonable procedures for compliance with provisions. No person may be held liable for any violation of subsection (a) or (b) of this section if he shows by a preponderance of the evidence that at the time of the violation he maintained reasonable procedures to assure compliance with subsection (a) or (b) of this section.

(d) Prohibitions.

(1) Certification. A consumer reporting agency shall not prepare or furnish investigative consumer report unless the agency has received a certification under subsection (a)(2) from the person who requested the report.

(2) Inquiries. A consumer reporting agency shall not make an inquiry for the purpose of preparing an investigative consumer report on a consumer for employment purposes if the making of the inquiry by an employer or prospective employer of the consumer would violate any applicable Federal or State equal employment opportunity law or regulation.

(3) Certain public record information. Except as otherwise provided in section 613 [§ 1681k], a consumer reporting agency shall not furnish an investigative consumer report that includes information that is a matter of public record and that relates to an arrest, indictment, conviction, civil judicial action, tax lien, or outstanding judgment, unless the agency has verified the accuracy of the information during the 30-day period ending on the date on which the report is furnished.

(4) Certain adverse information. A consumer reporting agency shall not prepare

or furnish an investigative consumer report on a consumer that contains information that is adverse to the interest of the consumer and that is obtained through a personal interview with a neighbor, friend, or associate of the consumer or with another person with whom the consumer is acquainted or who has knowledge of such item of information, unless

(A) the agency has followed reasonable procedures to obtain confirmation of the information, from an additional source that has independent and direct knowledge of the information; or

(B) the person interviewed is the best possible source of the information.

§ 607. Compliance procedures [15 U.S.C. § 1681e]

(a) Identity and purposes of credit users. Every consumer reporting agency shall maintain reasonable procedures designed to avoid violations of section 605 [§ 1681c] and to limit the furnishing of consumer reports to the purposes listed under section 604 [§ 1681b] of this title. These procedures shall require that prospective users of the information identify themselves, certify the purposes for which the information is sought, and certify that the information will be used for no other purpose. Every consumer reporting agency shall make a reasonable effort to verify the identity of a new prospective user and the uses certified by such prospective user prior to furnishing such user a consumer report. No consumer reporting agency may furnish a consumer report to any person if it has reasonable grounds for believing that the consumer report will not be used for a purpose listed in section 604 [§ 1681b] of this title.

(b) Accuracy of report. Whenever a consumer reporting agency prepares a consumer report it shall follow reasonable procedures to assure maximum possible accuracy of the information concerning the individual about whom the report relates.

(c) Disclosure of consumer reports by users allowed. A consumer reporting agency may not prohibit a user of a consumer report furnished by the agency on a consumer from disclosing the contents of the report to the consumer, if adverse action against the consumer has been taken by the user based in whole or in part on the report.

(d) Notice to users and furnishers of information.

(1) Notice requirement. A consumer reporting agency shall provide to any person

(A) who regularly and in the ordinary course of business furnishes information to the agency with respect to any consumer; or

(B) to whom a consumer report is provided by the agency;

a notice of such person's responsibilities under this title.

(2) Content of notice. The Federal Trade Commission shall prescribe the content of notices under paragraph (1), and a consumer reporting agency shall be in compliance with this subsection if it provides a notice under paragraph (1) that is substantially similar to the Federal Trade Commission prescription under this paragraph.

(e) Procurement of consumer report for resale.

(1) Disclosure. A person may not procure a consumer report for purposes of reselling the report (or any information in the report) unless the person discloses to the consumer reporting agency that originally furnishes the report

(A) the identity of the end-user of the report (or information); and

(B) each permissible purpose under section 604 [§ 1681b] for which the report is furnished to the end-user of the report (or information).

(2) Responsibilities of procurers for resale. A person who procures a consumer report for purposes of reselling the report (or any information in the report) shall

(A) establish and comply with reasonable procedures designed to ensure that the report (or information) is resold by the person only for a purpose for which the report may be furnished under section 604 [§ 1681b], including by requiring that each person to which the report (or information) is resold and that resells or provides the report (or information) to any other person

(i) identifies each end user of the resold report (or information);

(ii) certifies each purpose for which the report (or information) will be used; and

(iii) certifies that the report (or information) will be used for no other purpose; and

(B) before reselling the report, make reasonable efforts to verify the identifications and certifications made under subparagraph (A).

(3) Resale of consumer report to a federal agency or department. Notwithstanding paragraph (1) or (2), a person who procures a consumer report for purposes of reselling the report (or any information in the report) shall not disclose the identity of the end-user of the report under paragraph (1) or (2) if —

(A) the end user is an agency or department of the United States Government which procures the report from the person for purposes of determining the eligibility of the consumer concerned to receive access or continued access to classified information (as defined in section 604(b)(4)(E)(i)); and

(B) the agency or department certifies in writing to the person reselling the report that nondisclosure is necessary to protect classified information or the safety of persons employed by or contracting with, or undergoing investigation for work or contracting with the agency or department.

## § 608. Disclosures to governmental agencies [15 U.S.C. § 1681f]

Notwithstanding the provisions of section 604 [§ 1681b] of this title, a consumer reporting agency may furnish identifying information respecting any consumer, limited to his name, address, former addresses, places of employment, or former places of employment, to a governmental agency.

## § 609. Disclosures to consumers [15 U.S.C. § 1681g]

(a) Information on file; sources; report recipients. Every consumer reporting agency shall, upon request, and subject to 610(a)(1) [§ 1681h], clearly and accurately disclose to the consumer:

(1) All information in the consumer's file at the time of the request, except that nothing in this paragraph shall be construed to require a consumer reporting agency to disclose to a consumer any information concerning credit scores or any other risk scores or predictors relating to the consumer.

(2) The sources of the information; except that the sources of information acquired solely for use in preparing an investigative consumer report and actually used for no other purpose need not be disclosed: Provided, That in the event an action is brought under this title, such sources shall be available to the plaintiff under appropriate discovery procedures in the court in which the action is brought.

(3) (A) Identification of each person (including each end-user identified under section 607(e)(1) [§ 1681e]) that procured a consumer report

(i) for employment purposes, during the 2-year period preceding the date on which the request is made; or

(ii) for any other purpose, during the 1-year period preceding the date on which the request is made.

(B) An identification of a person under subparagraph (A) shall include

(i) the name of the person or, if applicable, the trade name (written in full) under which such person conducts business; and

(ii) upon request of the consumer, the address and telephone number of the person.

(C) Subparagraph (A) does not apply if—

(i) the end user is an agency or department of the United States Government that procures the report from the person for purposes of determining the eligibility of the consumer to whom the report relates to receive access or continued access to classified information (as defined in section 604(b)(4)(E)(i)); and

(ii) the head of the agency or department makes a written finding as prescribed under section 604(b)(4)(A).

(4) The dates, original payees, and amounts of any checks upon which is based any adverse characterization of the consumer, included in the file at the time of the disclosure.

(5) A record of all inquiries received by the agency during the 1-year period preceding the request that identified the consumer in connection with a credit or insurance transaction that was not initiated by the consumer.

(b) Exempt information. The requirements of subsection (a) of this section respecting the disclosure of sources of information and the recipients of consumer reports do not apply to information received or consumer reports furnished prior to the effective date of this title except to the extent that the matter involved is contained in the files of the consumer reporting agency on that date.

(c) Summary of rights required to be included with disclosure.

(1) Summary of rights. A consumer reporting agency shall provide to a consumer, with each written disclosure by the agency to the consumer under this section

(A) a written summary of all of the rights that the consumer has under this title; and

(B) in the case of a consumer reporting agency that compiles and maintains files on consumers on a nationwide basis, a toll-free telephone number established by the agency, at which personnel are accessible to consumers during normal business hours.

(2) Specific items required to be included. The summary of rights required under paragraph (1) shall include

(A) a brief description of this title and all rights of consumers under this title;

(B) an explanation of how the consumer may exercise the rights of the consumer under this title;

(C) a list of all Federal agencies responsible for enforcing any provision of this title and the address and any appropriate phone number of each such agency, in a form that will assist the consumer in selecting the appropriate agency;

(D) a statement that the consumer may have additional rights under State law and that the consumer may wish to contact a State or local consumer protection agency or a State attorney general to learn of those rights; and

(E) a statement that a consumer reporting agency is not required to remove accurate derogatory information from a consumer's file, unless the information is outdated under section 605 [§ 1681c] or cannot be verified.

(3) Form of summary of rights. For purposes of this subsection and any disclosure by a consumer reporting agency required under this title with respect to consumers' rights, the Federal Trade Commission (after consultation with each Federal agency referred to in section 621(b) [§ 1681s]) shall prescribe the form and content of any such disclosure of the rights of consumers required under this title. A consumer reporting agency shall be in compliance with this subsection if it provides disclosures under paragraph (1) that are substantially similar to the Federal Trade Commission prescription under this paragraph.

(4) Effectiveness. No disclosures shall be required under this subsection until the date on which the Federal Trade Commission prescribes the form and content of such disclosures under paragraph (3).

§ 610. Conditions and form of disclosure to consumers [15 U.S.C. § 1681h]

(a) In general.

(1) Proper identification. A consumer reporting agency shall require, as a condition of making the disclosures required under section 609 [§ 1681g], that the consumer furnish proper identification.

(2) Disclosure in writing. Except as provided in subsection (b), the disclosures required to be made under section 609 [§ 1681g] shall be provided under that section in writing.

(b) Other forms of disclosure.

(1) In general. If authorized by a consumer, a consumer reporting agency may make the disclosures required under 609 [§ 1681g]

(A) other than in writing; and

(B) in such form as may be

(i) specified by the consumer in accordance with paragraph (2); and

(ii) available from the agency.

(2) Form. A consumer may specify pursuant to paragraph (1) that disclosures under section 609 [§ 1681g] shall be made

(A) in person, upon the appearance of the consumer at the place of business of the consumer reporting agency where disclosures are regularly provided, during normal business hours, and on reasonable notice;

(B) by telephone, if the consumer has made a written request for disclosure by telephone;

(C) by electronic means, if available from the agency; or

(D) by any other reasonable means that is available from the agency.

(c) Trained personnel. Any consumer reporting agency shall provide trained personnel to explain to the consumer any information furnished to him pursuant to section 609 [§ 1681g] of this title.

(d) Persons accompanying consumer. The consumer shall be permitted to be accompanied by one other person of his choosing, who shall furnish reasonable identification. A consumer reporting agency may require the consumer to furnish a written statement granting permission to the consumer reporting agency to discuss the consumer's file in such person's presence.

(e) Limitation of liability. Except as provided in sections 616 and 617 [§§ 1681n and 1681o] of this title, no consumer may bring any action or proceeding in the nature of defamation, invasion of privacy, or negligence with respect to the reporting of information against any consumer reporting agency, any user of information, or any person who furnishes information to a consumer reporting agency, based on information disclosed pursuant to section 609, 610, or 615 [§§ 1681g, 1681h, or 1681m] of this title or based on information disclosed by a user of a consumer report to or for a consumer against whom the user has taken adverse action, based in whole or in part on the report, except as to false information furnished with malice or willful intent to injure such consumer.

§ 611. Procedure in case of disputed accuracy [15 U.S.C. § 1681i]

(a) Reinvestigations of disputed information.

(1) Reinvestigation required.

(A) In general. If the completeness or accuracy of any item of information contained in a consumer's file at a consumer reporting agency is disputed by the consumer and the consumer notifies the agency directly of such dispute, the agency shall reinvestigate free of charge and record the current status of the disputed information, or delete the item from the file in accordance with paragraph (5), before the end of the 30-day period beginning on the date on which the agency receives the notice of the dispute from the consumer.

(B) Extension of period to reinvestigate. Except as provided in subparagraph (C), the 30-day period described in subparagraph (A) may be extended for not more than 15 additional days if the consumer reporting agency receives information from the consumer during that 30-day period that is relevant to the reinvestigation.

(C) Limitations on extension of period to reinvestigate. Subparagraph (B) shall not apply to any reinvestigation in which, during the 30-day period described in subparagraph (A), the information that is the subject of the reinvestigation is found to be inaccurate or incomplete or the consumer reporting agency determines that the information cannot be verified.

(2) Prompt notice of dispute to furnisher of information.

(A) In general. Before the expiration of the 5-business-day period beginning on the date on which a consumer reporting agency receives notice of a dispute from any consumer in accordance with paragraph (1), the agency shall provide notification of the dispute to any person who provided any item of information in dispute, at the address and in the manner established with the person. The notice shall include all relevant information regarding the dispute that the agency has received from the consumer.

(B) Provision of other information from consumer. The consumer reporting agency shall promptly provide to the person who provided the information in dispute all relevant information regarding the dispute that is received by the agency from the consumer after the period referred to in subparagraph (A) and before the end of the period referred to in paragraph (1)(A).

(3) Determination that dispute is frivolous or irrelevant.

(A) In general. Notwithstanding paragraph (1), a consumer reporting agency may terminate a reinvestigation of information disputed by a consumer under that paragraph if the agency reasonably determines that the dispute by the consumer is frivolous or irrelevant, including by reason of a failure by a consumer to provide sufficient information to investigate the disputed information.

(B) Notice of determination. Upon making any determination in accordance with subparagraph (A) that a dispute is frivolous or irrelevant, a consumer reporting agency shall notify the consumer of such determination not later than 5 business days after making such determination, by mail or, if authorized by the consumer for that purpose, by any other means available to the agency.

(C) Contents of notice. A notice under subparagraph (B) shall include

(i) the reasons for the determination under subparagraph (A); and

(ii) identification of any information required to investigate the disputed information, which may consist of a standardized form describing the general nature of such information.

(4) Consideration of consumer information. In conducting any reinvestigation under paragraph (1) with respect to disputed information in the file of any consumer, the consumer reporting agency shall review and consider all relevant information submitted by the consumer in the period described in paragraph (1)(A) with respect

to such disputed information.

(5) Treatment of inaccurate or unverifiable information.

(A) In general. If, after any reinvestigation under paragraph (1) of any information disputed by a consumer, an item of the information is found to be inaccurate or incomplete or cannot be verified, the consumer reporting agency shall promptly delete that item of information from the consumer's file or modify that item of information, as appropriate, based on the results of the reinvestigation.

(B) Requirements relating to reinsertion of previously deleted material.

(i) Certification of accuracy of information. If any information is deleted from a consumer's file pursuant to subparagraph (A), the information may not be reinserted in the file by the consumer reporting agency unless the person who furnishes the information certifies that the information is complete and accurate.

(ii) Notice to consumer. If any information that has been deleted from a consumer's file pursuant to subparagraph (A) is reinserted in the file, the consumer reporting agency shall notify the consumer of the reinsertion in writing not later than 5 business days after the reinsertion or, if authorized by the consumer for that purpose, by any other means available to the agency.

(iii) Additional information. As part of, or in addition to, the notice under clause (ii), a consumer reporting agency shall provide to a consumer in writing not later than 5 business days after the date of the reinsertion

(I) a statement that the disputed information has been reinserted;

(II) the business name and address of any furnisher of information contacted and the telephone number of such furnisher, if reasonably available, or of any furnisher of information that contacted the consumer reporting agency, in connection with the reinsertion of such information; and

(III) a notice that the consumer has the right to add a statement to the consumer's file disputing the accuracy or completeness of the disputed information.

(C) Procedures to prevent reappearance. A consumer reporting agency shall maintain reasonable procedures designed to prevent the reappearance in a consumer's file, and in consumer reports on the consumer, of information that is deleted pursuant to this paragraph (other than information that is reinserted in accordance with subparagraph (B)(i)).

(D) Automated reinvestigation system. Any consumer reporting agency that compiles and maintains files on consumers on a nationwide basis shall implement an automated system through which furnishers of information to that consumer reporting agency may report the results of a reinvestigation that finds incomplete or inaccurate information in a consumer's file to other such consumer reporting agencies.

(6) Notice of results of reinvestigation.

(A) In general. A consumer reporting agency shall provide written notice to a consumer of the results of a reinvestigation under this subsection not later than 5 business days after the completion of the reinvestigation, by mail or, if authorized by the consumer for that purpose, by other means available to the agency.

(B) Contents. As part of, or in addition to, the notice under subparagraph (A), a consumer reporting agency shall provide to a consumer in writing before the expiration of the 5-day period referred to in subparagraph (A)

(i) a statement that the reinvestigation is completed;

(ii) a consumer report that is based upon the consumer's file as that file is revised as a result of the reinvestigation;

(iii) a notice that, if requested by the consumer, a description of the procedure used to determine the accuracy and completeness of the information shall be provided to the consumer by the agency, including the business name and address of any furnisher of information contacted in connection with such information and the telephone number of such furnisher, if reasonably available;

(iv) a notice that the consumer has the right to add a statement to the consumer's file disputing the accuracy or completeness of the information; and

(v) a notice that the consumer has the right to request under subsection (d) that the consumer reporting agency furnish notifications under that subsection.

(7) Description of reinvestigation procedure. A consumer reporting agency shall provide to a consumer a description referred to in paragraph (6)(B)(iii) by not later than 15 days after receiving a request from the consumer for that description.

(8) Expedited dispute resolution. If a dispute regarding an item of information in a consumer's file at a consumer reporting agency is resolved in accordance with paragraph (5)(A) by the deletion of the disputed information by not later than 3 business days after the date on which the agency receives notice of the dispute from the consumer in accordance with paragraph (1)(A), then the agency shall not be required to comply with paragraphs (2), (6), and (7) with respect to that dispute if the agency

(A) provides prompt notice of the deletion to the consumer by telephone;

(B) includes in that notice, or in a written notice that accompanies a confirmation and consumer report provided in accordance with subparagraph (C), a statement of the consumer's right to request under subsection (d) that the agency furnish notifications under that subsection; and

(C) provides written confirmation of the deletion and a copy of a consumer report on the consumer that is based on the consumer's file after the deletion, not later than 5 business days after making the deletion.

(b) Statement of dispute. If the reinvestigation does not resolve the dispute, the consumer may file a brief statement setting forth the nature of the dispute. The consumer reporting agency may limit such statements to not more than one hundred words if it provides the consumer with assistance in writing a clear summary of the dispute.

(c) Notification of consumer dispute in subsequent consumer reports. Whenever a statement of a dispute is filed, unless there is reasonable grounds to believe that it is frivolous or irrelevant, the consumer reporting agency shall, in any subsequent consumer report containing the information in question, clearly note that it is disputed by the consumer and provide either the consumer's statement or a clear and accurate codification or summary thereof.

(d) Notification of deletion of disputed information. Following any deletion of information which is found to be inaccurate or whose accuracy can no longer be verified or any notation as to disputed information, the consumer reporting agency shall, at the request of the consumer, furnish notification that the item has been deleted or the statement, codification or summary pursuant to subsection (b) or (c) of this section to any person specifically designated by the consumer who has within two years prior thereto received a consumer report for employment purposes, or within six months prior thereto received a consumer report for any other purpose, which contained the deleted or disputed information.

§ 612. Charges for certain disclosures [15 U.S.C. § 1681j]

(a) Reasonable charges allowed for certain disclosures.

(1) In general. Except as provided in subsections (b), (c), and (d), a consumer reporting agency may impose a reasonable charge on a consumer

(A) for making a disclosure to the consumer pursuant to section 609 [§ 1681g], which charge

(i) shall not exceed $8; and

(ii) shall be indicated to the consumer before making the disclosure; and

(B) for furnishing, pursuant to 611(d) [§ 1681i], following a reinvestigation under section 611(a) [§ 1681i], a statement, codification, or summary to a person designated by the consumer under that section after the 30-day period beginning on the date of notification of the consumer under paragraph (6) or (8) of section 611(a) [§ 1681i] with respect to the reinvestigation, which charge

(i) shall not exceed the charge that the agency would impose on each designated recipient for a consumer report; and

(ii) shall be indicated to the consumer before furnishing such information.

(2) Modification of amount. The Federal Trade Commission shall increase the amount referred to in paragraph (1)(A)(I) on January 1 of each year, based proportionally on changes in the Consumer Price Index, with fractional changes rounded to the nearest fifty cents.

(b) Free disclosure after adverse notice to consumer. Each consumer reporting agency that maintains a file on a consumer shall make all disclosures pursuant to section 609 [§ 1681g] without charge to the consumer if, not later than 60 days after receipt by such consumer of a notification pursuant to section 615 [§ 1681m], or of a notification from a debt collection agency affiliated with that consumer reporting agency stating that the consumer's credit rating may be or has been adversely affected, the consumer makes a request under section 609 [§ 1681g].

(c) Free disclosure under certain other circumstances. Upon the request of the consumer, a consumer reporting agency shall make all disclosures pursuant to section 609 [§ 1681g] once during any 12-month period without charge to that consumer if the consumer certifies in writing that the consumer

(1) is unemployed and intends to apply for employment in the 60-day period beginning on the date on which the certification is made;

(2) is a recipient of public welfare assistance; or

(3) has reason to believe that the file on the consumer at the agency contains inaccurate information due to fraud.

(d) Other charges prohibited. A consumer reporting agency shall not impose any charge on a consumer for providing any notification required by this title or making any disclosure required by this title, except as authorized by subsection (a).

§ 613. Public record information for employment purposes [15 U.S.C. § 1681k]

(a) In general. A consumer reporting agency which furnishes a consumer report for employment purposes and which for that purpose compiles and reports items of information on consumers which are matters of public record and are likely to have an adverse effect upon a consumer's ability to obtain employment shall

(1) at the time such public record information is reported to the user of such consumer report, notify the consumer of the fact that public record information is being reported by the consumer reporting agency, together with the name and address of the person to whom such information is being reported; or

(2) maintain strict procedures designed to insure that whenever public record information which is likely to have an adverse effect on a consumer's ability to obtain employment is reported it is complete and up to date. For purposes of this paragraph, items of public record relating to arrests, indictments, convictions, suits, tax liens, and

outstanding judgments shall be considered up to date if the current public record status of the item at the time of the report is reported.

(b) Exemption for national security investigations. Subsection (a) does not apply in the case of an agency or department of the United States Government that seeks to obtain and use a consumer report for employment purposes, if the head of the agency or department makes a written finding as prescribed under section 604(b)(4)(A).

§ 614. Restrictions on investigative consumer reports [15 U.S.C. § 1681l]

Whenever a consumer reporting agency prepares an investigative consumer report, no adverse information in the consumer report (other than information which is a matter of public record) may be included in a subsequent consumer report unless such adverse information has been verified in the process of making such subsequent consumer report, or the adverse information was received within the three-month period preceding the date the subsequent report is furnished.

§ 615. Requirements on users of consumer reports [15 U.S.C. § 1681m]

(a) Duties of users taking adverse actions on the basis of information contained in consumer reports. If any person takes any adverse action with respect to any consumer that is based in whole or in part on any information contained in a consumer report, the person shall

(1) provide oral, written, or electronic notice of the adverse action to the consumer;

(2) provide to the consumer orally, in writing, or electronically

(A) the name, address, and telephone number of the consumer reporting agency (including a toll-free telephone number established by the agency if the agency compiles and maintains files on consumers on a nationwide basis) that furnished the report to the person; and

(B) a statement that the consumer reporting agency did not make the decision to take the adverse action and is unable to provide the consumer the specific reasons why the adverse action was taken; and

(3) provide to the consumer an oral, written, or electronic notice of the consumer's right

(A) to obtain, under section 612 [§ 1681j], a free copy of a consumer report on the consumer from the consumer reporting agency referred to in paragraph (2), which notice shall include an indication of the 60-day period under that section for obtaining such a copy; and

(B) to dispute, under section 611 [§ 1681i], with a consumer reporting agency the accuracy or completeness of any information in a consumer report furnished by the agency.

(b) Adverse action based on information obtained from third parties other than consumer reporting agencies.

(1) In general. Whenever credit for personal, family, or household purposes involving a consumer is denied or the charge for such credit is increased either wholly or partly because of information obtained from a person other than a consumer reporting agency bearing upon the consumer's credit worthiness, credit standing, credit capacity, character, general reputation, personal characteristics, or mode of living, the user of such information shall, within a reasonable period of time, upon the consumer's written request for the reasons for such adverse action received within sixty days after learning of such adverse action, disclose the nature of the information to the consumer. The user of such information shall clearly and accurately disclose to the consumer his right to make such written request at the time such adverse action is communicated to the consumer.

(2) Duties of person taking certain actions based on information provided by affiliate.

(A) Duties, generally. If a person takes an action described in subparagraph (B) with respect to a consumer, based in whole or in part on information described in subparagraph (C), the person shall

(i) notify the consumer of the action, including a statement that the consumer may obtain the information in accordance with clause (ii); and

(ii) upon a written request from the consumer received within 60 days after transmittal of the notice required by clause (I), disclose to the consumer the nature of the information upon which the action is based by not later than 30 days after receipt of the request.

(B) Action described. An action referred to in subparagraph (A) is an adverse action described in section 603(k)(1)(A) [§ 1681a], taken in connection with a transaction initiated by the consumer, or any adverse action described in clause (i) or (ii) of section 603(k)(1)(B) [§ 1681a].

(C) Information described. Information referred to in subparagraph (A)

(i) except as provided in clause (ii), is information that

(I) is furnished to the person taking the action by a person related by common ownership or affiliated by common corporate control to the person taking the action; and

(II) bears on the credit worthiness, credit standing, credit capacity, character, general reputation, personal characteristics, or mode of living of the consumer; and

(ii) does not include

(I) information solely as to transactions or experiences between the consumer and the person furnishing the information; or

(II) information in a consumer report.

(c) Reasonable procedures to assure compliance. No person shall be held liable for any violation of this section if he shows by a preponderance of the evidence that at the time of the alleged violation he maintained reasonable procedures to assure compliance with the provisions of this section.

(d) Duties of users making written credit or insurance solicitations on the basis of information contained in consumer files.

(1) In general. Any person who uses a consumer report on any consumer in connection with any credit or insurance transaction that is not initiated by the consumer, that is provided to that person under section 604(c)(1)(B) [§ 1681b], shall provide with each written solicitation made to the consumer regarding the transaction a clear and conspicuous statement that

(A) information contained in the consumer's consumer report was used in connection with the transaction;

(B) the consumer received the offer of credit or insurance because the consumer satisfied the criteria for credit worthiness or insurability under which the consumer was selected for the offer;

(C) if applicable, the credit or insurance may not be extended if, after the consumer responds to the offer, the consumer does not meet the criteria used to select the consumer for the offer or any applicable criteria bearing on credit worthiness or insurability or does not furnish any required collateral;

(D) the consumer has a right to prohibit information contained in the consumer's file with any consumer reporting agency from being used in connection with any credit or insurance transaction that is not initiated by the consumer; and

(E) the consumer may exercise the right referred to in subparagraph (D) by notifying a notification system established under section 604(e) [§ 1681b].

(2) Disclosure of address and telephone number. A statement under paragraph (1) shall include the address and toll-free telephone number of the appropriate notification system established under section 604(e) [§ 1681b].

(3) Maintaining criteria on file. A person who makes an offer of credit or insurance to a consumer under a credit or insurance transaction described in paragraph (1) shall maintain on file the criteria used to select the consumer to receive the offer, all criteria bearing on credit worthiness or insurability, as applicable, that are the

basis for determining whether or not to extend credit or insurance pursuant to the offer, and any requirement for the furnishing of collateral as a condition of the extension of credit or insurance, until the expiration of the 3-year period beginning on the date on which the offer is made to the consumer.

(4) Authority of federal agencies regarding unfair or deceptive acts or practices not affected. This section is not intended to affect the authority of any Federal or State agency to enforce a prohibition against unfair or deceptive acts or practices, including the making of false or misleading statements in connection with a credit or insurance transaction that is not initiated by the consumer.

§ 616. Civil liability for willful noncompliance [15 U.S.C. § 1681n]

(a) In general. Any person who willfully fails to comply with any requirement imposed under this title with respect to any consumer is liable to that consumer in an amount equal to the sum of

(1) (A) any actual damages sustained by the consumer as a result of the failure or damages of not less than $100 and not more than $1,000; or

(B) in the case of liability of a natural person for obtaining a consumer report under false pretenses or knowingly without a permissible purpose, actual damages sustained by the consumer as a result of the failure or $1,000, whichever is greater;

(2) such amount of punitive damages as the court may allow; and

(3) in the case of any successful action to enforce any liability under this section, the costs of the action together with reasonable attorney's fees as determined by the court.

(b) Civil liability for knowing noncompliance. Any person who obtains a consumer report from a consumer reporting agency under false pretenses or knowingly without a permissible purpose shall be liable to the consumer reporting agency for actual damages sustained by the consumer reporting agency or $1,000, whichever is greater.

(c) Attorney's fees. Upon a finding by the court that an unsuccessful pleading, motion, or other paper filed in connection with an action under this section was filed in bad faith or for purposes of harassment, the court shall award to the prevailing party attorney's fees reasonable in relation to the work expended in responding to the pleading, motion, or other paper.

§ 617. Civil liability for negligent noncompliance [15 U.S.C. § 1681o]

(a) In general. Any person who is negligent in failing to comply with any requirement imposed under this title with respect to any consumer is liable to that consumer in an amount equal to the sum of

(1) any actual damages sustained by the consumer as a result of the failure;

(2) in the case of any successful action to enforce any liability under this section, the costs of the action together with reasonable attorney's fees as determined by the court.

(b) Attorney's fees. On a finding by the court that an unsuccessful pleading, motion, or other paper filed in connection with an action under this section was filed in bad faith or for purposes of harassment, the court shall award to the prevailing party attorney's fees reasonable in relation to the work expended in responding to the pleading, motion, or other paper.

§ 618. Jurisdiction of courts; limitation of actions [15 U.S.C. § 1681p]

An action to enforce any liability created under this title may be brought in any appropriate United States district court without regard to the amount in controversy, or in any other court of competent jurisdiction, within two years from the date on which the liability arises, except that where a defendant has materially and willfully misrepresented any information required under this title to be disclosed to an individual and the information so misrepresented is material to the establishment of the defendant's liability to that individual under this title, the action may be brought at any time within two years after discovery by the individual of the misrepresentation.

§ 619. Obtaining information under false pretenses [15 U.S.C. § 1681q]

Any person who knowingly and willfully obtains information on a consumer from a consumer reporting agency under false pretenses shall be fined under title 18, United States Code, imprisoned for not more than 2 years, or both.

§ 620. Unauthorized disclosures by officers or employees [15 U.S.C. § 1681r]

Any officer or employee of a consumer reporting agency who knowingly and willfully provides information concerning an individual from the agency's files to a person not authorized to receive that information shall be fined under title 18, United States Code, imprisoned for not more than 2 years, or both.

§ 621. Administrative enforcement [15 U.S.C. § 1681s]

(a) (1) Enforcement by Federal Trade Commission. Compliance with the requirements imposed under this title shall be enforced under the Federal Trade Commission Act [15 U.S.C. §§ 41 et seq.] by the Federal Trade Commission with respect to consumer reporting agencies and all other persons subject thereto, except to the extent that enforcement of the requirements imposed under this title is specifically committed to some other government agency under subsection (b) hereof. For the purpose of the exercise by the Federal Trade Commission of its functions and powers under the Federal Trade Commission Act, a violation of any requirement or prohibition imposed under this title shall constitute an unfair or deceptive act or practice in commerce in violation of section 5(a) of the Federal Trade Commission

Act [15 U.S.C. § 45(a)] and shall be subject to enforcement by the Federal Trade Commission under section 5(b) thereof [15 U.S.C. § 45(b)] with respect to any consumer reporting agency or person subject to enforcement by the Federal Trade Commission pursuant to this subsection, irrespective of whether that person is engaged in commerce or meets any other jurisdictional tests in the Federal Trade Commission Act. The Federal Trade Commission shall have such procedural, investigative, and enforcement powers, including the power to issue procedural rules in enforcing compliance with the requirements imposed under this title and to require the filing of reports, the production of documents, and the appearance of witnesses as though the applicable terms and conditions of the Federal Trade Commission Act were part of this title. Any person violating any of the provisions of this title shall be subject to the penalties and entitled to the privileges and immunities provided in the Federal Trade Commission Act as though the applicable terms and provisions thereof were part of this title.

2) (A) In the event of a knowing violation, which constitutes a pattern or practice of violations of this title, the Commission may commence a civil action to recover a civil penalty in a district court of the United States against any person that violates this title. In such action, such person shall be liable for a civil penalty of not more than $2,500 per violation.

(B) In determining the amount of a civil penalty under subparagraph (A), the court shall take into account the degree of culpability, any history of prior such conduct, ability to pay, effect on ability to continue to do business, and such other matters as justice may require.

(3) Notwithstanding paragraph (2), a court may not impose any civil penalty on a person for a violation of section 623(a)(1) [§ 1681s-2] unless the person has been enjoined from committing the violation, or ordered not to commit the violation, in an action or proceeding brought by or on behalf of the Federal Trade Commission, and has violated the injunction or order, and the court may not impose any civil penalty for any violation occurring before the date of the violation of the injunction or order.

(4) Neither the Commission nor any other agency referred to in subsection (b) may prescribe trade regulation rules or other regulations with respect to this title.

(b) Enforcement by other agencies. Compliance with the requirements imposed under this title with respect to consumer reporting agencies, persons who use consumer reports from such agencies, persons who furnish information to such agencies, and users of information that are subject to subsection (d) of section 615 [§ 1681m] shall be enforced under

(1) section 8 of the Federal Deposit Insurance Act [12 U.S.C. § 1818], in the case of

(A) national banks, and Federal branches and Federal agencies of foreign banks, by the Office of the Comptroller of the Currency;

(B) member banks of the Federal Reserve System (other than national banks), branches and agencies of foreign banks (other than Federal branches, Federal agencies, and insured State branches of foreign banks), commercial lending companies owned or controlled by foreign banks, and organizations operating under section 25 or 25(a) [25A] of the Federal Reserve Act [12 U.S.C. §§ 601 et seq., §§ 611 et seq], by the Board of Governors of the Federal Reserve System; and

(C) banks insured by the Federal Deposit Insurance Corporation (other than members of the Federal Reserve System) and insured State branches of foreign banks, by the Board of Directors of the Federal Deposit Insurance Corporation;

(2) section 8 of the Federal Deposit Insurance Act [12 U.S.C. § 1818], by the Director of the Office of Thrift Supervision, in the case of a savings association the deposits of which are insured by the Federal Deposit Insurance Corporation;

(3) the Federal Credit Union Act [12 U.S.C. §§ 1751 et seq.], by the Administrator of the National Credit Union Administration [National Credit Union Administration Board] with respect to any Federal credit union;

(4) subtitle IV of title 49 [49 U.S.C. §§ 10101 et seq.], by the Secretary of Transportation, with respect to all carriers subject to the jurisdiction of the Surface Transportation Board;

(5) the Federal Aviation Act of 1958 [49 U.S.C. Appx §§ 1301 et seq.], by the Secretary of Transportation with respect to any air carrier or foreign air carrier subject to that Act [49 U.S.C. Appx §§ 1301 et seq.]; and

(6) the Packers and Stockyards Act, 1921 [7 U.S.C. §§ 181 et seq.] (except as provided in section 406 of that Act [7 U.S.C. §§ 226 and 227]), by the Secretary of Agriculture with respect to any activities subject to that Act.

The terms used in paragraph (1) that are not defined in this title or otherwise defined in section 3(s) of the Federal Deposit Insurance Act (12 U.S.C. § 1813(s)) shall have the meaning given to them in section 1(b) of the International Banking Act of 1978 (12 U.S.C. § 3101).

(c) State action for violations.

(1) Authority of States. In addition to such other remedies as are provided under State law, if the chief law enforcement officer of a State, or an official or agency designated by a State, has reason to believe that any person has violated or is violating this title, the State

(A) may bring an action to enjoin such violation in any appropriate United States district court or in any other court of competent jurisdiction;

(B) subject to paragraph (5), may bring an action on behalf of the residents of the State to recover

(i) damages for which the person is liable to such residents under sections 616 and 617 [§§ 1681n and 1681o] as a result of the violation;

(ii) in the case of a violation of section 623(a) [§ 1681s-2], damages for which the person would, but for section 623(c) [§ 1681s-2], be liable to such residents as a result of the violation; or

(iii) damages of not more than $1,000 for each willful or negligent violation; and

(C) in the case of any successful action under subparagraph (A) or (B), shall be awarded the costs of the action and reasonable attorney fees as determined by the court.

(2) Rights of federal regulators. The State shall serve prior written notice of any action under paragraph (1) upon the Federal Trade Commission or the appropriate Federal regulator determined under subsection (b) and provide the Commission or appropriate Federal regulator with a copy of its complaint, except in any case in which such prior notice is not feasible, in which case the State shall serve such notice immediately upon instituting such action. The Federal Trade Commission or appropriate Federal regulator shall have the right

(A) to intervene in the action;

(B) upon so intervening, to be heard on all matters arising therein;

(C) to remove the action to the appropriate United States district court; and

(D) to file petitions for appeal.

(3) Investigatory powers. For purposes of bringing any action under this subsection, nothing in this subsection shall prevent the chief law enforcement officer, or an official or agency designated by a State, from exercising the powers conferred on the chief law enforcement officer or such official by the laws of such State to conduct investigations or to administer oaths or affirmations or to compel the attendance of witnesses or the production of documentary and other evidence.

(4) Limitation on State action while Federal action pending. If the Federal Trade Commission or the appropriate Federal regulator has instituted a civil action or an administrative action under section 8 of the Federal Deposit Insurance Act for a violation of this title, no State may, during the pendency of such action, bring an action under this section against any defendant named in the complaint of the Commission or the appropriate Federal regulator for any violation of this title that is alleged in that complaint.

(5) Limitations on state actions for violation of section 623(a)(1) [§ 1681s-2].

(A) Violation of injunction required. A State may not bring an action against a person under paragraph (1)(B) for a violation of section 623(a)(1) [§ 1681s-2], unless

(i) the person has been enjoined from committing the violation, in an action brought by the State under paragraph (1)(A); and

(ii) the person has violated the injunction.

(B) Limitation on damages recoverable. In an action against a person under paragraph (1)(B) for a violation of section 623(a)(1) [§ 1681s-2], a State may not recover any damages incurred before the date of the violation of an injunction on which the action is based.

(d) Enforcement under other authority. For the purpose of the exercise by any agency referred to in subsection (b) of this section of its powers under any Act referred to in that subsection, a violation of any requirement imposed under this title shall be deemed to be a violation of a requirement imposed under that Act. In addition to its powers under any provision of law specifically referred to in subsection (b) of this section, each of the agencies referred to in that subsection may exercise, for the purpose of enforcing compliance with any requirement imposed under this title any other authority conferred on it by law. Notwithstanding the preceding, no agency referred to in subsection (b) may conduct an examination of a bank, savings association, or credit union regarding compliance with the provisions of this title, except in response to a complaint (or if the agency otherwise has knowledge) that the bank, savings association, or credit union has violated a provision of this title, in which case, the agency may conduct an examination as necessary to investigate the complaint. If an agency determines during an investigation in response to a complaint that a violation of this title has occurred, the agency may, during its next 2 regularly scheduled examinations of the bank, savings association, or credit union, examine for compliance with this title.

(e) Interpretive authority. The Board of Governors of the Federal Reserve System may issue interpretations of any provision of this title as such provision may apply to any persons identified under paragraph (1), (2), and (3) of subsection (b), or to the holding companies and affiliates of such persons, in consultation with Federal agencies identified in paragraphs (1), (2), and (3) of subsection (b).

§ 622. Information on overdue child support obligations [15 U.S.C. § 1681s-1]

Notwithstanding any other provision of this title, a consumer reporting agency shall include in any consumer report furnished by the agency in accordance with section 604 [§ 1681b] of this title, any information on the failure of the consumer to pay overdue support which

(1) is provided

(A) to the consumer reporting agency by a State or local child support enforcement agency; or

(B) to the consumer reporting agency and verified by any local, State, or Federal government agency; and

(2) antedates the report by 7 years or less.

§ 623. Responsibilities of furnishers of information to consumer reporting agencies [15 U.S.C. § 1681s-2]

(a) Duty of furnishers of information to provide accurate information.

(1) Prohibition.

(A) Reporting information with actual knowledge of errors. A person shall not furnish any information relating to a consumer to any consumer reporting agency if the person knows or consciously avoids knowing that the information is inaccurate.

(B) Reporting information after notice and confirmation of errors. A person shall not furnish information relating to a consumer to any consumer reporting agency if

(i) the person has been notified by the consumer, at the address specified by the person for such notices, that specific information is inaccurate; and

(ii) the information is, in fact, inaccurate.

(C) No address requirement. A person who clearly and conspicuously specifies to the consumer an address for notices referred to in subparagraph (B) shall not be subject to subparagraph (A); however, nothing in subparagraph (B) shall require a person to specify such an address.

(2) Duty to correct and update information. A person who

(A) regularly and in the ordinary course of business furnishes information to one or more consumer reporting agencies about the person's transactions or experiences with any consumer; and

(B) has furnished to a consumer reporting agency information that the person determines is not complete or accurate,

shall promptly notify the consumer reporting agency of that determination and provide to the agency any corrections to that information, or any additional information, that is necessary to make the information provided by the person to the agency complete and accurate, and shall not thereafter furnish to the agency any of the information that remains not complete or accurate.

(3) Duty to provide notice of dispute. If the completeness or accuracy of any information furnished by any person to any consumer reporting agency is disputed to such person by a consumer, the person may not furnish the information to any consumer reporting agency without notice that such information is disputed by the consumer.

(4) Duty to provide notice of closed accounts. A person who regularly and in the ordinary course of business furnishes information to a consumer reporting agency regarding a consumer who has a credit account with that person shall notify the agency of the voluntary closure of the account by the consumer, in information regularly furnished for the period in which the account is closed.

(5) Duty to provide notice of delinquency of accounts. A person who furnishes information to a consumer reporting agency regarding a delinquent account being placed for collection, charged to profit or loss, or subjected to any similar action shall, not later than 90 days after furnishing the information, notify the agency of the month and year of the commencement of the delinquency that immediately preceded the action.

(b) Duties of furnishers of information upon notice of dispute.

(1) In general. After receiving notice pursuant to section 611(a)(2) [§ 1681i] of a dispute with regard to the completeness or accuracy of any information provided by a person to a consumer reporting agency, the person shall

(A) conduct an investigation with respect to the disputed information;

(B) review all relevant information provided by the consumer reporting agency pursuant to section 611(a)(2) [§ 1681i];

(C) report the results of the investigation to the consumer reporting agency; and

(D) if the investigation finds that the information is incomplete or inaccurate, report those results to all other consumer reporting agencies to which the person furnished the information and that compile and maintain files on consumers on a nationwide basis.

(2) Deadline. A person shall complete all investigations, reviews, and reports required under paragraph (1) regarding information provided by the person to a consumer reporting agency, before the expiration of the period under section 611(a)(1) [§ 1681i] within which the consumer reporting agency is required to complete actions required by that section regarding that information.

(c) Limitation on liability. Sections 616 and 617 [§§ 1681n and 1681o] do not apply to any failure to comply with subsection (a), except as provided in section 621(c)(1)(B) [§ 1681s].

(d) Limitation on enforcement. Subsection (a) shall be enforced exclusively under section 621 [§ 1681s] by the Federal agencies and officials and the State officials identified in that section.

§ 624. Relation to State laws [15 U.S.C. § 1681t]

(a) In general. Except as provided in subsections (b) and (c), this title does not annul, alter, affect, or exempt any person subject to the provisions of this title from complying with the laws of any State with respect to the collection, distribution, or use of any information on consumers, except to the extent that those laws are inconsistent with any provision of this title, and then only to the extent of the inconsistency.

(b) General exceptions. No requirement or prohibition may be imposed under the laws of any State

(1) with respect to any subject matter regulated under

(A) subsection (c) or (e) of section 604 [§ 1681b], relating to the prescreening of consumer reports;

(B) section 611 [§ 1681i], relating to the time by which a consumer reporting agency must take any action, including the provision of notification to a consumer or other person, in any procedure related to the disputed accuracy of information in a consumer's file, except that this subparagraph shall not apply to any State law in effect on the date of enactment of the Consumer Credit Reporting Reform Act of 1996;

(C) subsections (a) and (b) of section 615 [§ 1681m], relating to the duties of a person who takes any adverse action with respect to a consumer;

(D) section 615(d) [§ 1681m], relating to the duties of persons who use a consumer report of a consumer in connection with any credit or insurance transaction that is not initiated by the consumer and that consists of a firm offer of credit or insurance;

(E) section 605 [§ 1681c], relating to information contained in consumer reports, except that this subparagraph shall not apply to any State law in effect on the date of enactment of the Consumer Credit Reporting Reform Act of 1996; or

(F) section 623 [§ 1681s-2], relating to the responsibilities of persons who furnish information to consumer reporting agencies, except that this paragraph shall not apply

(i) with respect to section 54A(a) of chapter 93 of the Massachusetts Annotated Laws (as in effect on the date of enactment of the Consumer Credit Reporting Reform Act of 1996); or

(ii) with respect to section 1785.25(a) of the California Civil Code (as in effect on the date of enactment of the Consumer Credit Reporting Reform Act of 1996);

(2) with respect to the exchange of information among persons affiliated by common ownership or common corporate control, except that this paragraph shall not apply with respect to subsection (a) or (c)(1) of section 2480e of title 9, Vermont Statutes Annotated (as in effect on the date of enactment of the Consumer Credit

Reporting Reform Act of 1996); or

(3) with respect to the form and content of any disclosure required to be made under section 609(c) [§ 1681g].

(c) Definition of firm offer of credit or insurance. Notwithstanding any definition of the term "firm offer of credit or insurance" (or any equivalent term) under the laws of any State, the definition of that term contained in section 603(l) [§ 1681a] shall be construed to apply in the enforcement and interpretation of the laws of any State governing consumer reports.

(d) Limitations. Subsections (b) and (c)

(1) do not affect any settlement, agreement, or consent judgment between any State Attorney General and any consumer reporting agency in effect on the date of enactment of the Consumer Credit Reporting Reform Act of 1996; and

(2) do not apply to any provision of State law (including any provision of a State constitution) that

(A) is enacted after January 1, 2004;

(B) states explicitly that the provision is intended to supplement this title; and

(C) gives greater protection to consumers than is provided under this title.

§ 625. Disclosures to FBI for counterintelligence purposes [15 U.S.C. § 1681u]

(a) Identity of financial institutions. Notwithstanding section 604 [§ 1681b] or any other provision of this title, a consumer reporting agency shall furnish to the Federal Bureau of Investigation the names and addresses of all financial institutions (as that term is defined in section 1101 of the Right to Financial Privacy Act of 1978 [12 U.S.C. § 3401]) at which a consumer maintains or has maintained an account, to the extent that information is in the files of the agency, when presented with a written request for that information, signed by the Director of the Federal Bureau of Investigation, or the Director's designee, which certifies compliance with this section. The Director or the Director's designee may make such a certification only if the Director or the Director's designee has determined in writing that

(1) such information is necessary for the conduct of an authorized foreign counterintelligence investigation; and

(2) there are specific and articulable facts giving reason to believe that the consumer

(A) is a foreign power (as defined in section 101 of the Foreign Intelligence Surveillance Act of 1978 [50 U.S.C. § 1801]) or a person who is not a United States person (as defined in such section 101) and is an official of a foreign power; or

(B) is an agent of a foreign power and is engaging or has engaged in an act of international terrorism (as that term is defined in section 101(c) of the Foreign Intelligence Surveillance Act of 1978 [50 U.S.C. § 1801(c)]) or clandestine intelligence activities that involve or may involve a violation of criminal statutes of the United States.

(b) Identifying information. Notwithstanding the provisions of section 604 [§ 1681b] or any other provision of this title, a consumer reporting agency shall furnish identifying information respecting a consumer, limited to name, address, former addresses, places of employment, or former places of employment, to the Federal Bureau of Investigation when presented with a written request, signed by the Director or the Director's designee, which certifies compliance with this subsection. The Director or the Director's designee may make such a certification only if the Director or the Director's designee has determined in writing that

(1) such information is necessary to the conduct of an authorized counterintelligence investigation; and

(2) there is information giving reason to believe that the consumer has been, or is about to be, in contact with a foreign power or an agent of a foreign power (as defined in section 101 of the Foreign Intelligence Surveillance Act of 1978 [50 U.S.C. § 1801]).

(c) Court order for disclosure of consumer reports. Notwithstanding section 604 [§ 1681b] or any other provision of this title, if requested in writing by the Director of the Federal Bureau of Investigation, or a designee of the Director, a court may issue an order ex parte directing a consumer reporting agency to furnish a consumer report to the Federal Bureau of Investigation, upon a showing in camera that

(1) the consumer report is necessary for the conduct of an authorized foreign counterintelligence investigation; and

(2) there are specific and articulable facts giving reason to believe that the consumer whose consumer report is sought

(A) is an agent of a foreign power, and

(B) is engaging or has engaged in an act of international terrorism (as that term is defined in section 101(c) of the Foreign Intelligence Surveillance Act of 1978 [50 U.S.C. § 1801(c)]) or clandestine intelligence activities that involve or may involve a violation of criminal statutes of the United States.

The terms of an order issued under this subsection shall not disclose that the order is issued for purposes of a counterintelligence investigation.

(d) Confidentiality. No consumer reporting agency or officer, employee, or agent of a consumer reporting agency shall disclose to any person, other than those officers, employees, or agents of a consumer reporting agency necessary to fulfill the requirement to disclose information to the Federal Bureau of Investigation under this section, that the Federal Bureau of Investigation has sought or obtained the identity of financial institutions or a consumer report respecting any consumer under subsection (a), (b), or (c), and no consumer reporting agency or officer, employee, or agent of a consumer reporting agency shall include in any consumer report any information that would indicate that the Federal Bureau of Investigation has sought or obtained such information or a consumer report.

(e) Payment of fees. The Federal Bureau of Investigation shall, subject to the availability of appropriations, pay to the consumer reporting agency assembling or providing report or information in accordance with procedures established under this section a fee for reimbursement for such costs as are reasonably necessary and which have been directly incurred in searching, reproducing, or transporting books, papers, records, or other data required or requested to be produced under this section.

(f) Limit on dissemination. The Federal Bureau of Investigation may not disseminate information obtained pursuant to this section outside of the Federal Bureau of Investigation, except to other Federal agencies as may be necessary for the approval or conduct of a foreign counterintelligence investigation, or, where the information concerns a person subject to the Uniform Code of Military Justice, to appropriate investigative authorities within the military department concerned as may be necessary for the conduct of a joint foreign counterintelligence investigation.

(g) Rules of construction. Nothing in this section shall be construed to prohibit information from being furnished by the Federal Bureau of Investigation pursuant to a subpoena or court order, in connection with a judicial or administrative proceeding to enforce the provisions of this Act. Nothing in this section shall be construed to authorize or permit the withholding of information from the Congress.

(h) Reports to Congress. On a semiannual basis, the Attorney General shall fully inform the Permanent Select Committee on Intelligence and the Committee on Banking, Finance and Urban Affairs of the House of Representatives, and the Select Committee on Intelligence and the Committee on Banking, Housing, and Urban Affairs of the Senate concerning all requests made pursuant to subsections (a), (b), and (c).

(i) Damages. Any agency or department of the United States obtaining or disclosing any consumer reports, records, or information contained therein in violation of this section is liable to the consumer to whom such consumer reports, records, or information relate in an amount equal to the sum of

(1) $100, without regard to the volume of consumer reports, records, or information involved;

(2) any actual damages sustained by the consumer as a result of the disclosure;

(3) if the violation is found to have been willful or intentional, such punitive

damages as a court may allow; and

(4) in the case of any successful action to enforce liability under this subsection, the costs of the action, together with reasonable attorney fees, as determined by the court.

(j) Disciplinary actions for violations. If a court determines that any agency or department of the United States has violated any provision of this section and the court finds that the circumstances surrounding the violation raise questions of whether or not an officer or employee of the agency or department acted willfully or intentionally with respect to the violation, the agency or department shall promptly initiate a proceeding to determine whether or not disciplinary action is warranted against the officer or employee who was responsible for the violation.

(k) Good-faith exception. Notwithstanding any other provision of this title, any consumer reporting agency or agent or employee thereof making disclosure of consumer reports or identifying information pursuant to this subsection in good-faith reliance upon a certification of the Federal Bureau of Investigation pursuant to provisions of this section shall not be liable to any person for such disclosure under this title, the constitution of any State, or any law or regulation of any State or any political subdivision of any State.

(l) Limitation of remedies. Notwithstanding any other provision of this title, the remedies and sanctions set forth in this section shall be the only judicial remedies and sanctions for violation of this section.

(m) Injunctive relief. In addition to any other remedy contained in this section, injunctive relief shall be available to require compliance with the procedures of this section. In the event of any successful action under this subsection, costs together with reasonable attorney fees, as determined by the court, may be recovered.

---

Legislative History
House Reports: No. 91-975 (Comm. on Banking and Currency) and No. 91-1587 (Comm. of Conference)

Senate Reports: No. 91-1139 accompanying S. 3678 (Comm. on Banking and Currency)

Congressional Record, Vol. 116 (1970)

May 25, considered and passed House.
Sept. 18, considered and passed Senate, amended.
Oct. 9, Senate agreed to conference report.
Oct. 13, House agreed to conference report.

Enactment:
Public Law No. 91-508 (October 26, 1970):

Amendments: Public Law Nos.
95-473 (October 17, 1978)
95-598 (November 6, 1978)
98-443 (October 4, 1984)
101-73 (August 9, 1989)
102-242 (December 19, 1991)
102-537 (October 27, 1992)
102-550 (October 28, 1992)
103-325 (September 23, 1994)
104-88 (December 29, 1995)
104-93 (January 6, 1996)
104-193 (August 22, 1996)
104-208 (September 30, 1996)
105-107 (November 20, 1997)
105-347 (November 2, 1998)

---

1. The reporting periods have been lengthened for certain adverse information pertaining to U.S. Government insured or guaranteed student loans, or pertaining to national direct student loans. See sections 430A(f) and 463(c)(3) of the Higher Education Act of 1965, 20 U.S.C. 1080a(f) and 20 U.S.C. 1087cc(c)(3), respectively.

** Should read "paragraphs (4) and (5) ..." Prior Section 605(a)(6) was amended and redesignated as Section 605(a)(5) in November 1998.

▲

# THE FAIR DEBT COLLECTION PRACTICES ACT

As amended by Public Law 104-208, 110 Stat. 3009 (Sept. 30, 1996)

To amend the Consumer Credit Protection Act to prohibit abusive practices by debt collectors.

Be it enacted by the Senate and House of Representatives of the United States of America in Congress assembled, That the Consumer Credit Protection Act (15 U.S.C. 1601 et seq.) is amended by adding at the end thereof the following new title:

TITLE VIII—DEBT COLLECTION PRACTICES [Fair Debt Collection Practices Act]

§ 801. Short Title [15 USC 1601 note]

This title may be cited as the "Fair Debt Collection Practices Act."

§ 802. Congressional findings and declaration of purpose [15 USC 1692]

(a) There is abundant evidence of the use of abusive, deceptive, and unfair debt collection practices by many debt collectors. Abusive debt collection practices contribute to the number of personal bankruptcies, to marital instability, to the loss of jobs, and to invasions of individual privacy.

(b) Existing laws and procedures for redressing these injuries are inadequate to protect consumers.

(c) Means other than misrepresentation or other abusive debt collection practices are available for the effective collection of debts.

(d) Abusive debt collection practices are carried on to a substantial extent in interstate commerce and through means and instrumentalities of such commerce. Even where abusive debt collection practices are purely intrastate in character, they nevertheless directly affect interstate commerce.

(e) It is the purpose of this title to eliminate abusive debt collection practices by debt collectors, to insure that those debt collectors who refrain from using abusive debt collection practices are not competitively disadvantaged, and to promote consistent State action to protect consumers against debt collection abuses.

§ 803. Definitions [15 USC 1692a]

As used in this title —

(1) The term "Commission" means the Federal Trade Commission.

(2) The term "communication" means the conveying of information regarding a debt directly or indirectly to any person through any medium.

(3) The term "consumer" means any natural person obligated or allegedly obligated to pay any debt.

(4) The term "creditor" means any person who offers or extends credit creating a debt or to whom a debt is owed, but such term does not include any person to the

extent that he receives an assignment or transfer of a debt in default solely for the purpose of facilitating collection of such debt for another.

(5) The term "debt" means any obligation or alleged obligation of a consumer to pay money arising out of a transaction in which the money, property, insurance or services which are the subject of the transaction are primarily for personal, family, or household purposes, whether or not such obligation has been reduced to judgment.

(6) The term "debt collector" means any person who uses any instrumentality of interstate commerce or the mails in any business the principal purpose of which is the collection of any debts, or who regularly collects or attempts to collect, directly or indirectly, debts owed or due or asserted to be owed or due another. Notwithstanding the exclusion provided by clause (F) of the last sentence of this paragraph, the term includes any creditor who, in the process of collecting his own debts, uses any name other than his own which would indicate that a third person is collecting or attempting to collect such debts. For the purpose of section 808(6), such term also includes any person who uses any instrumentality of interstate commerce or the mails in any business the principal purpose of which is the enforcement of security interests. The term does not include—

(A) any officer or employee of a creditor while, in the name of the creditor, collecting debts for such creditor;

(B) any person while acting as a debt collector for another person, both of whom are related by common ownership or affiliated by corporate control, if the person acting as a debt collector does so only for persons to whom it is so related or affiliated and if the principal business of such person is not the collection of debts;

(C) any officer or employee of the United States or any State to the extent that collecting or attempting to collect any debt is in the performance of his official duties;

(D) any person while serving or attempting to serve legal process on any other person in connection with the judicial enforcement of any debt;

(E) any nonprofit organization which, at the request of consumers, performs bona fide consumer credit counseling and assists consumers in the liquidation of their debts by receiving payments from such consumers and distributing such amounts to creditors; and

(F) any person collecting or attempting to collect any debt owed or due or asserted to be owed or due another to the extent such activity (i) is incidental to a bona fide fiduciary obligation or a bona fide escrow arrangement; (ii) concerns a debt which was originated by such person; (iii) concerns a debt which was not in default at the time it was obtained by such person; or (iv) concerns a debt obtained by such person as a secured party in a commercial credit transaction involving the creditor.

(7) The term "location information" means a consumer's place of abode and his telephone number at such place, or his place of employment.

(8) The term "State" means any State, territory, or possession of the United

States, the District of Columbia, the Commonwealth of Puerto Rico, or any political subdivision of any of the foregoing.

## § 804. Acquisition of location information [15 USC 1692b]

Any debt collector communicating with any person other than the consumer for the purpose of acquiring location information about the consumer shall—

(1) identify himself, state that he is confirming or correcting location information concerning the consumer, and, only if expressly requested, identify his employer;

(2) not state that such consumer owes any debt;

(3) not communicate with any such person more than once unless requested to do so by such person or unless the debt collector reasonably believes that the earlier response of such person is erroneous or incomplete and that such person now has correct or complete location information;

(4) not communicate by post card;

(5) not use any language or symbol on any envelope or in the contents of any communication effected by the mails or telegram that indicates that the debt collector is in the debt collection business or that the communication relates to the collection of a debt; and

(6) after the debt collector knows the consumer is represented by an attorney with regard to the subject debt and has knowledge of, or can readily ascertain, such attorney's name and address, not communicate with any person other than that attorney, unless the attorney fails to respond within a reasonable period of time to the communication from the debt collector.

## § 805. Communication in connection with debt collection [15 USC 1692c]

(a) COMMUNICATION WITH THE CONSUMER GENERALLY. Without the prior consent of the consumer given directly to the debt collector or the express permission of a court of competent jurisdiction, a debt collector may not communicate with a consumer in connection with the collection of any debt—

(1) at any unusual time or place or a time or place known or which should be known to be inconvenient to the consumer. In the absence of knowledge of circumstances to the contrary, a debt collector shall assume that the convenient time for communicating with a consumer is after 8 o'clock antimeridian and before 9 o'clock postmeridian, local time at the consumer's location;

(2) if the debt collector knows the consumer is represented by an attorney with respect to such debt and has knowledge of, or can readily ascertain, such attorney's name and address, unless the attorney fails to respond within a reasonable period of time to a communication from the debt collector or unless the attorney consents to direct communication with the consumer; or

(3) at the consumer's place of employment if the debt collector knows or has reason to know that the consumer's employer prohibits the consumer from receiving such communication.

(b) COMMUNICATION WITH THIRD PARTIES. Except as provided in section 804, without the prior consent of the consumer given directly to the debt collector, or the express permission of a court of competent jurisdiction, or as reasonably necessary to effectuate a postjudgment judicial remedy, a debt collector may not communicate, in connection with the collection of any debt, with any person other than a consumer, his attorney, a consumer reporting agency if otherwise permitted by law, the creditor, the attorney of the creditor, or the attorney of the debt collector.

(c) CEASING COMMUNICATION. If a consumer notifies a debt collector in writing that the consumer refuses to pay a debt or that the consumer wishes the debt collector to cease further communication with the consumer, the debt collector shall not communicate further with the consumer with respect to such debt, except—

(1) to advise the consumer that the debt collector's further efforts are being terminated;

(2) to notify the consumer that the debt collector or creditor may invoke specified remedies which are ordinarily invoked by such debt collector or creditor; or

(3) where applicable, to notify the consumer that the debt collector or creditor intends to invoke a specified remedy.

If such notice from the consumer is made by mail, notification shall be complete upon receipt.

(d) For the purpose of this section, the term "consumer" includes the consumer's spouse, parent (if the consumer is a minor), guardian, executor, or administrator.

§ 806. Harassment or abuse [15 USC 1692d]

A debt collector may not engage in any conduct the natural consequence of which is to harass, oppress, or abuse any person in connection with the collection of a debt. Without limiting the general application of the foregoing, the following conduct is a violation of this section:

(1) The use or threat of use of violence or other criminal means to harm the physical person, reputation, or property of any person.

(2) The use of obscene or profane language or language the natural consequence of which is to abuse the hearer or reader.

(3) The publication of a list of consumers who allegedly refuse to pay debts, except to a consumer reporting agency or to persons meeting the requirements of section 603(f) or 604(3)1 of this Act.

(4) The advertisement for sale of any debt to coerce payment of the debt.

(5) Causing a telephone to ring or engaging any person in telephone conversation repeatedly or continuously with intent to annoy, abuse, or harass any person at the called number.

(6) Except as provided in section 804, the placement of telephone calls without meaningful disclosure of the caller's identity.

§ 807. False or misleading representations [15 USC 1962e]

A debt collector may not use any false, deceptive, or misleading representation or means in connection with the collection of any debt. Without limiting the general application of the foregoing, the following conduct is a violation of this section:

(1) The false representation or implication that the debt collector is vouched for, bonded by, or affiliated with the United States or any State, including the use of any badge, uniform, or facsimile thereof.

(2) The false representation of—

(A) the character, amount, or legal status of any debt; or

(B) any services rendered or compensation which may be lawfully received by any debt collector for the collection of a debt.

(3) The false representation or implication that any individual is an attorney or that any communication is from an attorney.

(4) The representation or implication that nonpayment of any debt will result in the arrest or imprisonment of any person or the seizure, garnishment, attachment, or sale of any property or wages of any person unless such action is lawful and the debt collector or creditor intends to take such action.

(5) The threat to take any action that cannot legally be taken or that is not intended to be taken.

(6) The false representation or implication that a sale, referral, or other transfer of any interest in a debt shall cause the consumer to—

(A) lose any claim or defense to payment of the debt; or

(B) become subject to any practice prohibited by this title.

(7) The false representation or implication that the consumer committed any crime or other conduct in order to disgrace the consumer.

(8) Communicating or threatening to communicate to any person credit information which is known or which should be known to be false, including the failure to communicate that a disputed debt is disputed.

(9) The use or distribution of any written communication which simulates or is falsely represented to be a document authorized, issued, or approved by any court,

official, or agency of the United States or any State, or which creates a false impression as to its source, authorization, or approval.

(10) The use of any false representation or deceptive means to collect or attempt to collect any debt or to obtain information concerning a consumer.

(11) The failure to disclose in the initial written communication with the consumer and, in addition, if the initial communication with the consumer is oral, in that initial oral communication, that the debt collector is attempting to collect a debt and that any information obtained will be used for that purpose, and the failure to disclose in subsequent communications that the communication is from a debt collector, except that this paragraph shall not apply to a formal pleading made in connection with a legal action.

(12) The false representation or implication that accounts have been turned over to innocent purchasers for value.

(13) The false representation or implication that documents are legal process.

(14) The use of any business, company, or organization name other than the true name of the debt collector's business, company, or organization.

(15) The false representation or implication that documents are not legal process forms or do not require action by the consumer.

(16) The false representation or implication that a debt collector operates or is employed by a consumer reporting agency as defined by section 603(f) of this Act.

§ 808. Unfair practices [15 USC 1692f]

A debt collector may not use unfair or unconscionable means to collect or attempt to collect any debt. Without limiting the general application of the foregoing, the following conduct is a violation of this section:

(1) The collection of any amount (including any interest, fee, charge, or expense incidental to the principal obligation) unless such amount is expressly authorized by the agreement creating the debt or permitted by law.

(2) The acceptance by a debt collector from any person of a check or other payment instrument postdated by more than five days unless such person is notified in writing of the debt collector's intent to deposit such check or instrument not more than ten nor less than three business days prior to such deposit.

(3) The solicitation by a debt collector of any postdated check or other postdated payment instrument for the purpose of threatening or instituting criminal prosecution.

(4) Depositing or threatening to deposit any postdated check or other postdated payment instrument prior to the date on such check or instrument.

(5) Causing charges to be made to any person for communications by conceal-

ment of the true propose of the communication. Such charges include, but are not limited to, collect telephone calls and telegram fees.

(6) Taking or threatening to take any nonjudicial action to effect dispossession or disablement of property if—

(A) there is no present right to possession of the property claimed as collateral through an enforceable security interest;

(B) there is no present intention to take possession of the property; or

(C) the property is exempt by law from such dispossession or disablement.

(7) Communicating with a consumer regarding a debt by post card.

(8) Using any language or symbol, other than the debt collector's address, on any envelope when communicating with a consumer by use of the mails or by telegram, except that a debt collector may use his business name if such name does not indicate that he is in the debt collection business.

§ 809. Validation of debts [15 USC 1692g]

(a) Within five days after the initial communication with a consumer in connection with the collection of any debt, a debt collector shall, unless the following information is contained in the initial communication or the consumer has paid the debt, send the consumer a written notice containing—

(1) the amount of the debt;

(2) the name of the creditor to whom the debt is owed;

(3) a statement that unless the consumer, within thirty days after receipt of the notice, disputes the validity of the debt, or any portion thereof, the debt will be assumed to be valid by the debt collector;

(4) a statement that if the consumer notifies the debt collector in writing within the thirty-day period that the debt, or any portion thereof, is disputed, the debt collector will obtain verification of the debt or a copy of a judgment against the consumer and a copy of such verification or judgment will be mailed to the consumer by the debt collector; and

(5) a statement that, upon the consumer's written request within the thirty-day period, the debt collector will provide the consumer with the name and address of the original creditor, if different from the current creditor.

(b) If the consumer notifies the debt collector in writing within the thirty-day period described in subsection (a) that the debt, or any portion thereof, is disputed, or that the consumer requests the name and address of the original creditor, the debt collector shall cease collection of the debt, or any disputed portion thereof, until the debt collector obtains verification of the debt or any copy of a judgment, or the name and address of the original creditor, and a copy of such verification or judgment, or name and address of the original creditor, is mailed to the consumer by the debt collector.

(c) The failure of a consumer to dispute the validity of a debt under this section may not be construed by any court as an admission of liability by the consumer.

## § 810. Multiple debts [15 USC 1692h]

If any consumer owes multiple debts and makes any single payment to any debt collector with respect to such debts, such debt collector may not apply such payment to any debt which is disputed by the consumer and, where applicable, shall apply such payment in accordance with the consumer's directions.

## § 811. Legal actions by debt collectors [15 USC 1692i]

(a) Any debt collector who brings any legal action on a debt against any consumer shall—

(1) in the case of an action to enforce an interest in real property securing the consumer's obligation, bring such action only in a judicial district or similar legal entity in which such real property is located; or

(2) in the case of an action not described in paragraph (1), bring such action only in the judicial district or similar legal entity—

(A) in which such consumer signed the contract sued upon; or

(B) in which such consumer resides at the commencement of the action.

(b) Nothing in this title shall be construed to authorize the bringing of legal actions by debt collectors.

## § 812. Furnishing certain deceptive forms [15 USC 1692j]

(a) It is unlawful to design, compile, and furnish any form knowing that such form would be used to create the false belief in a consumer that a person other than the creditor of such consumer is participating in the collection of or in an attempt to collect a debt such consumer allegedly owes such creditor, when in fact such person is not so participating.

(b) Any person who violates this section shall be liable to the same extent and in the same manner as a debt collector is liable under section 813 for failure to comply with a provision of this title.

## § 813. Civil liability [15 USC 1692k]

(a) Except as otherwise provided by this section, any debt collector who fails to comply with any provision of this title with respect to any person is liable to such person in an amount equal to the sum of—

(1) any actual damage sustained by such person as a result of such failure;

(2) (A) in the case of any action by an individual, such additional damages as the court may allow, but not exceeding $1,000; or

(B) in the case of a class action, (i) such amount for each named plaintiff as could be recovered under subparagraph (A), and (ii) such amount as the court may allow for all other class members, without regard to a minimum individual recovery, not to exceed the lesser of $500,000 or 1 per centum of the net worth of the debt collector; and

(3) in the case of any successful action to enforce the foregoing liability, the costs of the action, together with a reasonable attorney's fee as determined by the court. On a finding by the court that an action under this section was brought in bad faith and for the purpose of harassment, the court may award to the defendant attorney's fees reasonable in relation to the work expended and costs.

(b) In determining the amount of liability in any action under subsection (a), the court shall consider, among other relevant factors—

(1) in any individual action under subsection (a)(2)(A), the frequency and persistence of noncompliance by the debt collector, the nature of such noncompliance, and the extent to which such noncompliance was intentional; or

(2) in any class action under subsection (a)(2)(B), the frequency and persistence of noncompliance by the debt collector, the nature of such noncompliance, the resources of the debt collector, the number of persons adversely affected, and the extent to which the debt collector's noncompliance was intentional.

(c) A debt collector may not be held liable in any action brought under this title if the debt collector shows by a preponderance of evidence that the violation was not intentional and resulted from a bona fide error notwithstanding the maintenance of procedures reasonably adapted to avoid any such error.

(d) An action to enforce any liability created by this title may be brought in any appropriate United States district court without regard to the amount in controversy, or in any other court of competent jurisdiction, within one year from the date on which the violation occurs.

(e) No provision of this section imposing any liability shall apply to any act done or omitted in good faith in conformity with any advisory opinion of the Commission, notwithstanding that after such act or omission has occurred, such opinion is amended, rescinded, or determined by judicial or other authority to be invalid for any reason.

§ 814. Administrative enforcement [15 USC 1692l]

(a) Compliance with this title shall be enforced by the Commission, except to the extend that enforcement of the requirements imposed under this title is specifically committed to another agency under subsection (b). For purpose of the exercise by the Commission of its functions and powers under the Federal Trade Commission Act, a violation of this title shall be deemed an unfair or deceptive act or practice in violation of that Act. All of the functions and powers of the Commission under the

Federal Trade Commission Act are available to the Commission to enforce compliance by any person with this title, irrespective of whether that person is engaged in commerce or meets any other jurisdictional tests in the Federal Trade Commission Act, including the power to enforce the provisions of this title in the same manner as if the violation had been a violation of a Federal Trade Commission trade regulation rule.

(b) Compliance with any requirements imposed under this title shall be enforced under—

(1) section 8 of the Federal Deposit Insurance Act, in the case of—

(A) national banks, by the Comptroller of the Currency;

(B) member banks of the Federal Reserve System (other than national banks), by the Federal Reserve Board; and

(C) banks the deposits or accounts of which are insured by the Federal Deposit Insurance Corporation (other than members of the Federal Reserve System), by the Board of Directors of the Federal Deposit Insurance Corporation;

(2) section 5(d) of the Home Owners Loan Act of 1933, section 407 of the National Housing Act, and sections 6(i) and 17 of the Federal Home Loan Bank Act, by the Federal Home Loan Bank Board (acting directing or through the Federal Savings and Loan Insurance Corporation), in the case of any institution subject to any of those provisions;

(3) the Federal Credit Union Act, by the Administrator of the National Credit Union Administration with respect to any Federal credit union;

(4) subtitle IV of Title 49, by the Interstate Commerce Commission with respect to any common carrier subject to such subtitle;

(5) the Federal Aviation Act of 1958, by the Secretary of Transportation with respect to any air carrier or any foreign air carrier subject to that Act; and

(6) the Packers and Stockyards Act, 1921 (except as provided in section 406 of that Act), by the Secretary of Agriculture with respect to any activities subject to that Act.

(c) For the purpose of the exercise by any agency referred to in subsection (b) of its powers under any Act referred to in that subsection, a violation of any requirement imposed under this title shall be deemed to be a violation of a requirement imposed under that Act. In addition to its powers under any provision of law specifically referred to in subsection (b), each of the agencies referred to in that subsection may exercise, for the purpose of enforcing compliance with any requirement imposed under this title any other authority conferred on it by law, except as provided in subsection (d).

(d) Neither the Commission nor any other agency referred to in subsection (b) may promulgate trade regulation rules or other regulations with respect to the collection of debts by debt collectors as defined in this title.

§ 815. Reports to Congress by the Commission [15 USC 1692m]

(a) Not later than one year after the effective date of this title and at one-year intervals thereafter, the Commission shall make reports to the Congress concerning the administration of its functions under this title, including such recommendations as the Commission deems necessary or appropriate. In addition, each report of the Commission shall include its assessment of the extent to which compliance with this title is being achieved and a summary of the enforcement actions taken by the Commission under section 814 of this title.

(b) In the exercise of its functions under this title, the Commission may obtain upon request the views of any other Federal agency which exercises enforcement functions under section 814 of this title.

§ 816. Relation to State laws [15 USC 1692n]

This title does not annul, alter, or affect, or exempt any person subject to the provisions of this title from complying with the laws of any State with respect to debt collection practices, except to the extent that those laws are inconsistent with any provision of this title, and then only to the extent of the inconsistency. For purposes of this section, a State law is not inconsistent with this title if the protection such law affords any consumer is greater than the protection provided by this title.

§ 817. Exemption for State regulation [15 USC 1692o]

The Commission shall by regulation exempt from the requirements of this title any class of debt collection practices within any State if the Commission determines that under the law of that State that class of debt collection practices is subject to requirements substantially similar to those imposed by this title, and that there is adequate provision for enforcement.

§ 818. Effective date [15 USC 1692 note]

This title takes effect upon the expiration of six months after the date of its enactment, but section 809 shall apply only with respect to debts for which the initial attempt to collect occurs after such effective date.

Approved September 20, 1977

---

ENDNOTES

1. So in original; however, should read "604(a)(3)."

LEGISLATIVE HISTORY:

Public Law 95-109 [H.R. 5294]

HOUSE REPORT No. 95-131 (Comm. on Banking, Finance, and Urban Affairs).

SENATE REPORT No. 95-382 (Comm. on Banking, Housing, and Urban Affairs).

CONGRESSIONAL RECORD, Vol. 123 (1977):

Apr. 4, considered and passed House.

Aug. 5, considered and passed Senate, amended.

Sept. 8, House agreed to Senate amendment.

WEEKLY COMPILATION OF PRESIDENTIAL DOCUMENTS, Vol. 13, No. 39:

Sept. 20, Presidential statement.

AMENDMENTS:

SECTION 621, SUBSECTIONS (b)(3), (b)(4) and (b)(5) were amended to transfer certain administrative enforcement responsibilities, pursuant to Pub. L. 95-473, § 3(b), Oct. 17, 1978. 92 Stat. 166; Pub. L. 95-630, Title V. § 501, November 10, 1978, 92 Stat. 3680; Pub. L. 98-443, § 9(h), Oct. 4, 1984, 98 Stat. 708.

SECTION 803, SUBSECTION (6), defining "debt collector," was amended to repeal the attorney at law exemption at former Section (6)(F) and to redesignate Section 803(6)(G) pursuant to Pub. L. 99-361, July 9, 1986, 100 Stat. 768. For legislative history, see H.R. 237, HOUSE REPORT No. 99-405 (Comm. on Banking, Finance and Urban Affairs). CONGRESSIONAL RECORD: Vol. 131 (1985): Dec. 2, considered and passed House. Vol. 132 (1986): June 26, considered and passed Senate.

SECTION 807, SUBSECTION (11), was amended to affect when debt collectors must state (a) that they are attempting to collect a debt and (b) that information obtained will be used for that purpose, pursuant to Pub. L. 104-208 § 2305, 110 Stat. 3009 (Sept. 30, 1996).

▲

# THE FAIR CREDIT
# BILLING ACT

### § 301. Short Title

This title may be cited as the "Fair Credit Billing Act."

### § 302. Declaration of purpose

The last sentence of section 102 of the Truth in Lending Act (15 U.S.C. 1601) is amended by striking out the period and inserting in lieu thereof a comma and the following: "and to protect the consumer against inaccurate and unfair credit billing and credit card practices."

### § 303. Definitions of creditor and open end credit plan

The first sentence of section 103(f) of the Truth in Lending Act (15 U.S.C. 1602(f)) is amended to read as follows: "The term 'creditor' refers only to creditors who regularly extend, or arrange for the extension of, credit which is payable by agreement in more than four installments or for which the payment of a finance charge is or may be required, whether in connection with loans, sales of property or services, or otherwise. For the purposes of the requirements imposed under Chapter 4 and sections 127(a) (6), 127(a) (7), 127(a) (8), 127(b) (1), 127(b) (2), 127(b) (3), 127(b) (9), and 127(b) (11) of Chapter 2 of this Title, the term 'creditor' shall also include card issuers whether or not the amount due is payable by agreement in more than four installments or the payment of a finance charge is or may be required, and the Board shall, by regulation, apply these requirements to such card issuers, to the extent appropriate, even though the requirements are by their terms applicable only to creditors offering open end credit plans.

### § 304. Disclosure of fair credit billing rights

(a) Section 127(a) of the Truth in Lending Act (15 U.S.C. 1637(a)) is amended by adding at the end thereof a new paragraph as follows:

"(8) A statement, in a form prescribed by regulations of the Board      o f the protection provided by sections 161 and 170 to an obligor      and the creditor's responsibilities under sections 162 and 170.      With respect to each of two billing cycles per year, at semiannual  intervals, the creditor shall transmit such statement to each obligor to whom the creditor is required to transmit a statement pursuant to sections 127(b) for such billing cycle."

(b) Section 127(c) of such Act (15 U.S.C. 1637(c)) is amended to read:

"(c) In the case of any existing account under an open end consumer credit plan having an outstanding balance of more than $1 at or after the close of the creditor's first full billing cycle under the plan after the effective date of subsection (a) or any amendments thereto, the items described in subsection (a), to the extent applicable and not previously disclosed, shall be disclosed     in a notice mailed or delivered to the obligor not later than the time of mailing the next statement required by subsection (b)."

### § 305. Disclosure of billing contact

Section 127(b) of the Truth in Lending Act (15 U.S.C. 1637(b)) is amended by adding at the end thereof a new paragraph as follows:

"(11) The address to be used by the creditor for the purpose of receiving billing inquiries from the obligor."

### § 306. Billing practices

The Truth in Lending Act (15 U.S.C. 1601-1665) is amended by adding at the end thereof a new chapter as follows:

### Chapter 4—CREDIT BILLING

Sec.
161. Correction of billing errors.
162. Regulation of credit reports.
163. Length of billing period.
164. Prompt crediting of payments.
165. Crediting excess payments.
166. Prompt notification of returns.
167. Use of cash discounts.
168. Prohibition of tie-in services.
169. Prohibition of offsets.
170. Rights of credit card customers.
171. Relation to State laws.

### § 161. Correction of billing errors

"(a) If a creditor, within sixty days after having transmitted to an obligor a statement of the obligor's account in connection with an extension of consumer credit, receives at the address disclosed under section 127(b) (11) a written notice (other than notice on a payment stub or other payment medium supplied by the creditor if the creditor so stipulates with the disclosure required under section 127(a) (8) from the obligor in which the obligor—

"(1) sets forth or otherwise enables the creditor to identify the name and account number (if any) of the obligor,

"(2) indicates the obligor's belief that the statement contains a billing error and the amount of such billing error, and

"(3) sets forth the reasons for the obligor's belief (to the extent applicable) that the statement contains a billing error, the creditor shall, unless the obligor has, after giving such written notice and before the expiration of the time limits herein specified, agreed that the statement was correct—

"(A) not later than thirty days after the receipt of the notice, send a written acknowledgment thereof to the obligor, unless the action required in subparagraph (B) is taken within such thirty-day period, and

"(B) not later than two complete billing cycles of the creditor (in no event later than ninety days) after the receipt of the notice and prior to taking any action to collect the amount, or any part thereof, indicated by the obligor under paragraph (2) either—

"(i) make appropriate corrections in the account of the obligor, including the crediting of any finance charges on amounts erroneously billed, and transmit to the obligor a notification of such corrections and the creditor's explanation of any cage in the amount indicated by the obligor under paragraph (2) and, if any such change is made and the obligor so requests, copies of documentary evidence of the obligor's indebtedness; or

"(ii) send a written explanation or clarification to the obligor, after having conducted an investigation, setting forth to the extent applicable the reasons why the creditor believes the account of the obligor was correctly shown in the statement and, upon request of the obligor, provide copies of documentary evidence of the obligor's indebtedness. In the case of a billing error where the obligor alleges that the creditor's billing statement reflects goods not delivered to the obligor or his designee in accordance with the agreement made at the time of the transaction, a creditor may not construe such amount to be correctly shown unless he determines that such goods were actually delivered, mailed, or otherwise sent to the obligor and provides the obligor with a statement of such determination.

After complying with the provisions of this subsection with respect to an alleged billing error, a creditor has no further responsibility under this section if the obligor continues to make substantially the same allegation with respect to such error.

"(b) For the purpose of this section, a 'billing error' consists of any of the following:

"(1) A reflection on a statement of an extension of credit which was not made to the obligor or, if made, was not in the amount reflected on such statement.

"(2) A reflection on a statement of an extension of credit for which the obligor requests additional clarification including documentary evidence thereof.

"(3) A reflection on a statement of goods or services not accepted by the obligor or his designee or not delivered to the obligor or his designee in accordance with the agreement made at the time of a transaction.

"(4) The creditor's failure to reflect properly on a statement a payment made by the obligor or a credit issued to the obligor.

"(5) A computation error or similar error of an accounting nature of the creditor on a statement.

"(6) Any other error described in regulations of the Board.

"(c) For the purposes of this section, action to collect the amount, or any part thereof, indicated by an obligor under paragraph (2)™ does not include the sending of statements of account to the obligor following written notice from the obligor as specified under subsection (a) if—

"(1) the obligor's account is not restricted or closed because of the failure of the obligor to pay the amount indicated under paragraph (2) of subsection (a) and

"(2) the creditor indicates the payment of such amount is not required pending the creditor's compliance with this section.

Nothing in this section shall be construed to prohibit any action by a creditor to collect any amount which has not been indicated by the obligor to contain a billing error.

"(d) Pursuant to regulations of the Board, a creditor operating an open end consumer credit plan may not, prior to the sending of the written explanation or clarification required under paragraph (B) (ii), restrict or close an account with respect to which the obligor has indicated pursuant to subsection (a) that he believes such account to contain a billing error solely because of the obligor's failure to pay the amount indicated to be in error. Nothing in this subsection shall be deemed to prohibit a creditor from applying against the credit limit on the obligor's account the amount indicated to be in error.

"(e) Any creditor who fails to comply with the requirements of this section or section 162 forfeits any right to collect from the obligor the amount indicated by the obligor under paragraph (2) of subsection (a) of this section, and any finance charges thereon, except that the amount required to be forfeited under this subsection may not exceed $50.

### § 162. Regulation of credit reports

"(a) After receiving a notice from an obligor as provided in section 161(a), a creditor or his agent may not directly or indirectly threaten to report to any person adversely on the obligor's credit rating or credit standing because of the obligor's failure to pay the amount indicated by the obligor under section 161(a) (2) and such amount may not be reported as delinquent to any third party until the creditor has met the requirements of section 161 and has allowed the obligor the same number of days (not less than ten) thereafter to make payment as is provided under the credit agreement with the obligor for the payment of undisputed amounts.

"(b) If a creditor receives a further written notice from an obligor that an amount is still in dispute within the time allowed for payment under subsection (a) of this section, a creditor may not report to any third party that the amount of the obligor is delinquent because the obligor has failed to pay an amount which he has indicated under section 161(a) (2), unless the creditor also reports that the amount is in dispute and, at the same time, notifies the obligor of the name and address of each party to whom the creditor is reporting information concerning the delinquency.

"(c) A creditor shall report any subsequent resolution of any delinquencies reported pursuant to subsection (b) to the parties to whom such delinquencies were initially reported.

### § 163. Length of billing period

"(a) If an open end consumer credit plan provides a time period within which an obligor may repay any portion of the credit extended without incurring an additional finance charge, such additional finance charge may not be imposed with respect to such portion of the credit extended for the billing cycle of which such period is a part unless a statement which includes the amount upon which the finance charge for that period is based was mailed at least fourteen days prior to the date specified in the statement by which payment must be made in order to avoid imposition of that finance charge.

"(b) Subsection (a) does not apply in any case where a creditor has been prevented, delayed, or hindered in making timely mailing or delivery of such periodic statement within the time period specified in such subsection because of an act of God, war, natural disaster, strike, or other excusable or justifiable cause, as determined under regulations of the Board.

### § 164. Prompt crediting of payments
"Payments received from an obligor under an open end consumer credit plan by the creditor shall be posted promptly to the obligor's account as specified in regulations of the Board. Such regulations shall prevent a finance charge from being imposed on any obligor if the creditor has received the obligor's payment in readily identifiable form in the amount, manner, location, and time indicated by the creditor to avoid the imposition thereof.

### § 165. Crediting excess payments
"Whenever an obligor transmits funds to a creditor in excess of the total balance due on an open end consumer credit account, the creditor shall promptly (1) upon request of the obligor refund the amount of the overpayment, or (2) credit such amount to the obligor's account.

### § 166. Prompt notification of returns
"With respect to any sales transaction where a credit card has been used to obtain credit, where the seller is a person other than the card issuer, and where the seller accepts or allows a return of the goods or forgiveness of a debit for services which were the subject of such sale, the seller shall promptly transmit to the credit card issuer, a credit statement with respect thereto and the credit card issuer shall credit the account of the obligor for the amount of the transaction.

### § 167. Use of cash discounts
"(a) With respect to credit card which may be used for extensions of credit in sales transactions in which the seller is a person other than the card issuer, the card issuer may not, by contract or otherwise, prohibit any such seller from offering a discount to a cardholder to induce the cardholder to pay by cash, check, or similar means rather than use a credit card.

"(b) With respect to any sales transaction, any discount not in excess of 5 per centum offered by the seller for the purpose of inducing payment by cash, check, or other means not involving the use of a credit card shall not constitute a finance charge as determined under section 106, if such discount is offered to all prospective buyers and its availability is disclosed to all prospective buyers clearly and conspicuously in accordance with regulations of the Board.

### § 168. Prohibition of tie-in services
"Notwithstanding any agreement to the contrary, a card issuer may not require a seller, as a condition to participating in a credit card plan, to open an account with or procure any other service from the card issuer or its subsidiary or agent.

### § 169. Prohibition of offsets

"(a) A card issuer may not take any action to offset a cardholder's indebtedness arising in connection with a consumer credit transaction under the relevant credit card plan against funds of the cardholder held on deposit with the card issuer unless—

"(1) such action was previously authorized in writing by the cardholder in accordance with a credit plan whereby the cardholder agrees periodically to pay debts incurred in his open end credit account by permitting the card issuer periodically to deduct all or a portion of such debt from the cardholder's deposit account, and

"(2) such action with respect to any outstanding disputed amount not be taken by the card issuer upon request of the cardholder.

In the case of any credit card account in existence on the effective date of this section, the previous written authorization referred to in clause (1) shall not be required until the date (after such effective date) when such account is renewed, but in no case later than one year after such effective date. Such written authorization shall be deemed to exist if the card issuer has previously notified the cardholder that the use of his credit card account will subject any funds which the card issuer holds in deposit accounts of such cardholder to offset against any amounts due and payable on his credit card account which have not been paid in accordance with the terms of the agreement between the card issuer and the cardholder.

"(b) This section does not alter or affect the right under State law of a card issuer to attach or otherwise levy upon funds of a cardholder held on deposit with the card issuer if that remedy is constitutionally available to creditors generally.

### § 170. Rights of credit card customers

"(a) Subject to the limitation contained in subsection (b), a card issuer who has issued a credit card to a cardholder pursuant to an open end consumer credit plan shall be subject to all claims (other than tort claims) and defenses arising out of any transaction in which the credit card is used as a method of payment or extension of credit if (1) the obligor has made a good faith attempt to obtain satisfactory resolution of a disagreement or problem relative to the transaction from the person honoring the credit card; (2) the amount of the initial transaction exceeds $50; and (3) the place where the initial transaction occurred was in the same State as the mailing address previously provided by the cardholder or was within 100 miles from such address, except that the limitations set forth in clauses (2) and (3) with respect to an obligor's right to assert claims and defenses against a card issuer shall not be applicable to any transaction in which the person honoring the credit card (A) is the same person as the card issuer, (B) is controlled by the card issuer, (C) is under direct or indirect common control with the card issuer, (D) is a franchised dealer in the card issuer's products or services, or (E) has obtained the order for such transaction through a mail solicitation made by or participated in by the card issuer in which the cardholder is solicited to enter into such transaction by using the credit card issued by the card issuer.

"(b) The amount of claims or defenses asserted by the cardholder may not exceed the amount of credit outstanding with respect to such transaction at the time the cardholder first notifies the card issuer or the person honoring the credit card of such claim or defense. For the purpose of determining the amount of credit outstanding in the preceding sentence, payments and credits to the cardholder's account are deemed to have been applied, in the order indicated, to the payment of:

(1) late charges in the order of their entry to the account; (2) finance charges in order of their entry to the account; and (3) debits to the account other than those set

forth above, in the order in which each debit entry to the account was made.

## § 171. Relation to State laws

"(a) This chapter does not annul, alter, or affect, or exempt any person subject to the provisions of this chapter from complying with, the laws of any State with respect to credit billing practices, except to the extent that those laws are inconsistent with any provision of this chapter, and then only to the extent of the inconsistency. The Board is authorized to determine whether such inconsistencies exist. The Board may not determine that any State law is inconsistent with any provision of this chapter if the Board determines that such law gives greater protection to the consumer.

"(b) The Board shall by regulation exempt from the requirements of this chapter any class of credit transactions within any State if it determines that under the law of that State that class of transactions is subject to requirements substantially similar to those imposed under this chapter or that such law gives greater protection to the consumer, and that there is adequate provision for enforcement."

## § 307. Conforming amendments

(a) The table of chapter of the Truth in Lending Act is amended by adding immediately under item 3 the following:

"4. CREDIT BILLING . . . . . . . . . . . . . . . . . . . . . . . . 1611"

(b) Section 111(d) of such Act (15 U.S.C. 1610(d)) is amended by striking out "and 130" and inserting in lieu thereof a comma and the following: "130, and 166"

(c) Section 121(a) of such Act (15 U.S.C. 1631(a)) is amended—

(1) by striking out "and upon whom a finance charge is or may be imposed"; and

(2) by inserting "or chapter 4" immediately after "this chapter".

(d) Section 121(b) of such Act (15 U.S.C. 1631(b)) is amended by inserting "or chapter 4" immediately after "this chapter".

(e) Section 122(a) of such Act (15 U.S.C. 1632(a)) is amended by inserting "or chapter 4" immediately after "this chapter".

(f) Section 122(b) of such Act (15 U.S.C. 1632(b)) is amended by inserting "or chapter 4" immediately after "this chapter".

## § 308. Effective date

This title takes effect upon the expiration of one year after the date of its enactment.

▲

# GETTING APPROVED UNDER ADVERSE CONDITIONS

## AUTO LOAN

The best place to get an auto loan under adverse credit conditions is through Ford Motor Credit. Ford wants to sell cars any way it can and has the most lenient terms available for buyers of its automobiles. Even after you've filed bankruptcy, Ford will likely approve you.

## CREDIT CARDS

The problem with building credit is the need for unsecured credit cards. Many issuers of secured cards report them as such. But a couple of issuers will provide a secured card but report it as unsecured, and even extend you more credit than your secured deposit. I recommend that you look into the secured cards from Capital One (www.capitalone.com) and American Pacific Bank (www.apbank.com).

## OTHER RESOURCES

### bankrate.com

Bankrate.com is a veritable plethora of information, and you will find the best rates available on any type of loan on this Web site.

### bestcredit.com

At Bestcredit we're always looking to provide better ways to get you on your way to relief, so log onto bestcredit.com and see what new products and services are available.

### Federal Trade Commission

The FTC offers many resources, such as the latest rules and guidelines to debt collecting and credit reporting. Its Web site is www.ftc.gov

# ▲
# ABOUT THE
# AUTHOR

In the early 1980s, Dana Neal learned all of the tricks of the trade while collecting for the Greater Lakes Higher Education Corporation. He quickly became disenchanted with the way his peers conducted themselves and with the state of credit reporting in the United States in general.

After graduating from Ohio State University in 1991 with a degree in aviation, he went on to active duty, piloting several types of aircraft, including the UH-60 Blackhawk helicopter and various multiengine airplanes.

After being injured in the line of duty and medically retired from service, he became a consumer advocate. His mission: to inform others of their rights and to demonstrate that they wield significant power over their credit report. In keeping with that goal, he founded Bestcredit in 1999. He now spends his time teaching others what his experience as both a collector and a debtor taught him about debt collection and credit reporting.